CORBA
Security

The Addison-Wesley Object Technology Series

Grady Booch, Ivar Jacobson, and James Rumbaugh, Series Editors
For more information check out the series web site [http://www.awl.com /cseng/otseries/] as well as the pages
on each book [http://www.awl.com/cseng/I-S-B-N/] (I-S-B-N represents the actual ISBN, including dashes).

David Bellin and Susan Suchman Simone, *The CRC Card Book*,
ISBN 0-201-89535-8

Robert V. Binder, *Testing Object-Oriented Systems: Models,
Patterns, and Tools*, ISBN 0-201-80938-9

Bob Blakley, *CORBA Security: An Introduction to Safe
Computing with Objects*, ISBN 0-201-32565-9

Grady Booch, *Object Solutions: Managing the Object-Oriented
Project*, ISBN 0-8053-0594-7

Grady Booch, *Object-Oriented Analysis and Design with
Applications, Second Edition*, ISBN 0-8053-5340-2

Grady Booch, James Rumbaugh, and Ivar Jacobson, *The Unified
Modeling Language User Guide*, ISBN 0-201-57168-4

Don Box, *Essential COM*, ISBN 0-201-63446-5

Don Box, Keith Brown, Tim Ewald, and Chris Sells, *Effective
COM: 50 Ways to Improve Your COM and MTS-based
Applications*, ISBN 0-201-37968-6

Alistair Cockburn, *Surviving Object-Oriented Projects: A
Manager's Guide*, ISBN 0-201-49834-0

Dave Collins, *Designing Object-Oriented User Interfaces*,
ISBN 0-8053-5350-X

Jim Conallen, *Building Web Applications with UML*,
ISBN 0-201-61577-0

Bruce Powel Douglass, *Doing Hard Time: Designing and
Implementing Embedded Systems with UML*,
ISBN 0-201-49837-5

Bruce Powel Douglass, *Real-Time UML, Second Edition:
Developing Efficient Objects for Embedded Systems*,
ISBN 0-201-65784-8

Desmond F. D'Souza and Alan Cameron Wills, *Objects,
Components, and Frameworks with UML: The Catalysis
Approach*, ISBN 0-201-31012-0

Martin Fowler, *Analysis Patterns: Reusable Object Models*,
ISBN 0-201-89542-0

Martin Fowler, *Refactoring: Improving the Design of Existing
Code*, ISBN 0-201-48567-2

Martin Fowler with Kendall Scott, *UML Distilled, Second
Edition: Applying the Standard Object Modeling Language*,
ISBN 0-201-65783-X

Peter Heinckiens, *Building Scalable Database Applications:
Object-Oriented Design, Architectures, and Implementations*,
ISBN 0-201-31013-9

Christine Hofmeister, Robert Nord, Soni Dilip, *Applied Software
Architecture*, ISBN 0-201-32571-3

Ivar Jacobson, Grady Booch, and James Rumbaugh, *The Unified
Software Development Process*, ISBN 0-201-57169-2

Ivar Jacobson, Magnus Christerson, Patrik Jonsson, and Gunnar
Overgaard, *Object-Oriented Software Engineering: A Use Case
Driven Approach*, ISBN 0-201-54435-0

Ivar Jacobson, Maria Ericsson, and Agneta Jacobson, *The Object
Advantage: Business Process Reengineering with Object
Technology*, ISBN 0-201-42289-1

Ivar Jacobson, Martin Griss, and Patrik Jonsson, *Software Reuse:
Architecture, Process and Organization for Business Success*,
ISBN 0-201-92476-5

David Jordan, *C++ Object Databases: Programming with the
ODMG Standard*, ISBN 0-201-63488-0

Philippe Kruchten, *The Rational Unified Process: An
Introduction*, ISBN 0-201-60459-0

Wilf LaLonde, *Discovering Smalltalk*, ISBN 0-8053-2720-7

Dean Leffingwell and Don Widrig, *Managing Software
Requirements: A Unified Approach*, ISBN 0-201-61593-2

Chris Marshall, *Enterprise Modeling with UML:
Designing Successful Software through Business Analysis*,
ISBN 0-201-43313-3

Lockheed Martin Advanced Concepts Center and Rational
Software Corporation, *Succeeding with the Booch and OMT
Methods: A Practical Approach*, ISBN 0-8053-2279-5

Thomas Mowbray and William Ruh, *Inside CORBA: Distributed
Object Standards and Applications*, ISBN 0-201-89540-4

Bernd Oestereich, *Developing Software with UML: Object-
Oriented Analysis and Design in Practice*, ISBN 0-201-39826-5

Meiler Page-Jones, *Fundamentals of Object-Oriented Design in
UML*, ISBN 0-201-69946-X

Ira Pohl, *Object-Oriented Programming Using C++, Second
Edition*, ISBN 0-201-89550-1

Rob Pooley and Perdita Stevens, *Using UML: Software
Engineering with Objects and Components*, ISBN 0-201-36067-5

Terry Quatrani, *Visual Modeling with Rational Rose 2000
and UML*, ISBN 0-201-69961-3

Brent E. Rector and Chris Sells, *ATL Internals*,
ISBN 0-201-69589-8

Paul R. Reed, Jr., *Developing Applications with Visual Basic
and UML*, ISBN 0-201-61579-7

Doug Rosenberg with Kendall Scott, *Use Case Driven Object
Modeling with UML: A Practical Approach*, ISBN 0-201-43289-7

Walker Royce, *Software Project Management: A Unified
Framework*, ISBN 0-201-30958-0

William Ruh, Thomas Herron, and Paul Klinker, *IIOP Complete:
Middleware Interoperability and Distributed Object Standards*,
ISBN 0-201-37925-2

James Rumbaugh, Ivar Jacobson, and Grady Booch, *The Unified
Modeling Language Reference Manual*, ISBN 0-201-30998-X

Geri Schneider and Jason P. Winters, *Applying Use Cases:
A Practical Guide*, ISBN 0-201-30981-5

Yen-Ping Shan and Ralph H. Earle, *Enterprise Computing with
Objects: From Client/Server Environments to the Internet*,
ISBN 0-201-32566-7

David N. Smith, *IBM Smalltalk: The Language*,
ISBN 0-8053-0908-X

Daniel Tkach, Walter Fang, and Andrew So, *Visual Modeling
Technique: Object Technology Using Visual Programming*,
ISBN 0-8053-2574-3

Daniel Tkach and Richard Puttick, *Object Technology in
Application Development, Second Edition*, ISBN 0-201-49833-2

Jos Warmer and Anneke Kleppe, *The Object Constraint
Language: Precise Modeling with UML*, ISBN 0-201-37940-6

CORBA
Security

An Introduction to
Safe Computing with Objects

Bob Blakley

ADDISON-WESLEY

An imprint of Addison Wesley Longman, Inc.

Reading, Massachusetts • Harlow, England • Menlo Park, California

Berkeley, California • Don Mills, Ontario • Sydney

Bonn • Amsterdam • Tokyo • Mexico City

The publisher offers discounts on this book when ordered in quantity for special sales. For more information, please contact:

AWL Direct Sales
Addison Wesley Longman, Inc.
One Jacob Way
Reading, Massachusetts 01867
(781) 944-3700

Visit AWL on the Web: www.awl.com/cseng/

Library of Congress Cataloging-in-Publication Data

Blakley, Bob, 1960-
  CORBA security: an introduction to safe computing with objects/Bob Blakley.
    p. cm. -- (Addison-Wesley object technology series)
  Includes bibliographical references
  ISBN 0-201-32565-9 (alk. paper)
   1. Computer Security. 2. CORBA (Computer architecture) 3. Object-oriented methods
(Computer science) I. Title. II. Series.

  QA76.9.A25 B58 1999
  005.8--dc21   99040091

Executive Editor: J. Carter Shanklin
Project Editor: Krysia Bebick
Editorial Assistant: Kristin Erickson
Production Manager: Sarah Weaver
Cover Design: Simone R. Payment
Compositor: GEX Publishing Services

ISBN 0-201-32565-9

Text printed on recycled and acid-free paper
1 2 3 4 5 6 7 8 9 10—MA—03 02 01 00 99
First printing, October 1999

Contents

1.
Objects and Security

2.
Object Security

3.
Policy

4.
Identification, Authentication, and Privilege

5.
Access Control

6.
Message Protection

7.
Delegation

List of Figures

Foreword

It has been well understood for centuries that abstraction lies at the heart of human design and construction of complex systems. The only way that we can understand, structure, and teach about complex systems is to find everyday metaphors for generalizations of system design.

In the computer science field, we generally like our abstractions layered. Disregarding the fact that in most scientific and engineering fields layering of abstractions is uncommon, we prefer to say that level "one" sits squarely atop layer "two," "two" entirely atop "three," and "three" completely obscuring "four." We know, as practitioners, that the new level "zero" will not only use "one" but take quick peeks at "two" through "four"—but we try not to talk about it, turning our embarrassed faces away from the whiteboard. The reasons are always excellent—the performance requirement is the most common one—but the resulting tangle (especially in long-term maintenance) is always painful.

The most famous example of a carefully designed layered abstraction in the computer systems security realm must be the Multics operating system. I had the fantastic luck to be involved, in a small way at the beginning of my career, with Multics system programming for several years at MIT and then at Honeywell. We were well aware that this was the most secure system around (as well as having the best-designed multi-layer memory system, but that's another foreword!), with security designed in from day one rather than pasted in afterwards.

Unfortunately, most of the project members were also aware that the layered security model of Multics was wrong! Although it was rigorously enforced, it did not model well the real-world security issues of (for example) principles of equal security access level, but different access based on need-to-know. It assumed for the most part a strictly layered "ring 7" down to "ring 0" set of security levels, enforced by the hardware and checked by the software at every turn.

Fast-forward to the 1990s, and we find an international consortium (the Object Management Group, or OMG) designing abstractions and system orthogonalities to simplify the rather complex life of the world community of enterprise-wide heterogeneous system developers. Since 1989, the OMG has been defining software interfaces and design rules to make large-system design more portable, more interoperable, and simply more possible. The Unified Modeling Language (UML) for designing complex systems and the Common Object Request Broker Architecture (CORBA) for connecting disparate systems, OMG's best-known specifications, were defined by an open, neutral, consensus-making process comprised (at this writing) of some 800 member companies from around the world.

The CORBA specification was originally completed in 1991. Since that time it has integrated many important new trends in the industry—the Web, the Java language, application server technology, and so forth—without changing its basic structure, design, and architecture. More importantly, it has constantly grown layered services (called CORBAservices in OMG's parlance) for simplifying the life of the distributed application developer.

The strength of the open, neutral, industry-wide consensus-making approach is that it draws together the best in the industry, all of the experts, to focus on specific problems. In 1994 and 1995, as part of what was to become known as the CORBA 2.0 process, the world's best distributed systems experts from many different organizations (including industry, academia, and government) came together to create the new CORBAsecurity specification.

The completed specification when published would be called the best and most ambitious distributed system security standard in the industry by the Technical Director of the U.S. National Security Agency's Information Systems Security Organization. Nevertheless, careful revision management would upgrade this specification in 1997 and 1999. This is an important orthogonality to get right, for government (such as military) as well as private (such as healthcare) organizations. Nevertheless, while important, this CORBAsecurity service is only a part of a much larger whole.

In a sense, one could characterize OMG's efforts (which at this point have expanded to application areas from telecommunications and healthcare to life sciences and satellite systems) as a search for abstractions in the object universe. OMG's efforts are founded on a belief in the object-oriented approach to system design, not only because of the good modeling match between object orientation and real-world systems, but also because object-oriented systems better model non-layered systems.

A glance at the OMG foundation Object Management Architecture (OMA) finds the metaphoric treatment of CORBA as a "backplane" or "software bus" that connects components across the enterprise. While individual components may be layered internally, there is no restriction that when piled together there is a *de jure* (or even *de facto*) layering. Rather, large, complex, enterprise-wide systems are considered a cooperating set of components. This is a good match (metaphorically) to what the enterprise itself is: a set of cooperating people, with abstraction layers (organizational chart reporting structure) often changing and never simple.

Unfortunately, this throws our nice, neat set of software orthogonalities into a tizzy. How are we to understand the maintenance of transactional integrity, persistence requirements, and secure communications and storage when we can only view such functionality as services on par with our own application-specific components? In terms of security, which parts of such a system must be physically secured? Where are the fences and gates?

You will find a wealth of answers to your security questions in this clear and concise examination of the many aspects of security addressed by the CORBAsecurity service. Starting from base principles of object models and security concepts, Bob Blakley builds up all of the complex ideas of modern secure systems, from authentication and encryption to non-repudiation for the commercial and military worlds. Clear examples and straightforward language outline the requirements and common-sense structures that make building secure systems possible, with a modicum of orthogonality. Although we will never be able to fully abstract everything, we do have to continue to try!

Richard Mark Soley, Ph.D.
Chairman and CEO
Object Management Group, Inc.
August 1999

Preface

This book will introduce you to security in object-oriented environments. It doesn't assume any background in security, and it assumes only a general familiarity with object-oriented systems.

This is an introductory book

There are a lot of books on computer security; some of the author's favorites are listed in the bibliography. Most of them are written by experts, for experts. They tend to contain lots of detailed explanations of encryption systems (like RSA) and security protocols (like Kerberos), or they focus on how to build secure operating system kernels or secure databases. Many of these books are very good; people who need to build secure systems couldn't, or at least shouldn't, live without them.

Many security books have a "bits up" perspective

If you aren't a security expert, but you do need to understand and use secure systems, you have fewer resources to turn to.

This book looks at security from a "policy-down" perspective

There aren't a lot of books that tell you what a secure system which someone else has already built looks like "from the outside" or how to use such a system to protect yourself and your data. This book tries to do that. It approaches security from the viewpoint of policy—what you want your secure system to allow and to forbid — rather than from the viewpoint of the mechanisms which enforce the policy. Policy is what you see when you tell the system what the rules are, and it's what the bad guys see when they get the "access denied" message.

This book is not an in-depth study. It presents object security at a "concept" level and omits many of the details. There are no scary C++ programs; there aren't even any trendy Java programs! There are lots of pictures and real-world examples of how secure object

It's not too technical

systems can be used to enforce interesting and useful security policies. There's a minimum of jargon, and the jargon that just couldn't be eliminated is explained in the glossary. There is also a "running summary" in the outer margin of each page which you can read to get an overview of the main points in the book if you're in a hurry.

If you're a manager, this book will teach you what you need to know about security issues and options in object-oriented environments, without a lot of unnecessary technical detail.

If you're a security administrator, this book should help you figure out what policies are reasonable in object-oriented environments and how object security technology can help you define, manage, and enforce those policies.

If you're considering buying or implementing an object-oriented system and you want to know what the risks are and what you can do to protect yourself, this book will help you answer those questions.

But it's still very useful to technical people

Most programmers aren't security experts. If you're in this category and you need to get up to speed on object security, you should find the book very useful, because it approaches the problem at a conceptual level. If you are a security expert, but you aren't familiar with the unique security problems which arise in object-oriented environments, there's something here for you, too.

Finally, if you're a CORBA programmer (keep reading if you don't know what this means), this book is a good introduction to the OMG CORBAsecurity specification, which is notoriously hard to read.

The object security model described in this book is based on CORBAsecurity. CORBA is the OMG's Common Object Request Broker Architecture. It describes an "object bus" through which applications can talk to objects. An implementation of the CORBA object bus is called an Object Request Broker (or ORB).

It's based on CORBA security

CORBAsecurity defines a set of security services which can be used to protect objects (and messages sent to objects) in a CORBA environment. The CORBAsecurity specification was produced by a large group of the industry's top security experts. It's recently been revised to add new features and to clean up a few of the inevitable small defects which creep into the first release of a specification.

The author was one of the two editors of the CORBAsecurity specification and is a member of the revision committee, so you're getting the inside story.

The CORBAsecurity model was designed to allow ORB vendors to build the model using any of a variety of existing security technologies, and different vendors are in fact using different technologies "under the covers" in their implementations.

But the security model it describes is very general

The CORBAsecurity model could be used to protect almost any object-oriented system. For example, it could be used to protect Java objects, ActiveX objects, or Smalltalk objects, though it hasn't been implemented in any of these environments yet.

The book concludes with a useful list of questions to ask vendors who say their object systems are secure. The questions will help you figure out what protection an object-oriented system provides and how strong that protection is.

The book ends with a list of follow-up questions

Acknowledgments

I'd like to thank a lot of people for their help and support, both during the creation of the OMG CORBAsecurity specification and during the writing of this book.

The CORBAsecurity architecture was created by the members of "the Gonville Group": Lance Allred, Christian Ammon, Bob Hagman, Bret Hartman, Richard Herbert, Anne Hopkins, Ken McCoy, Chris Milsom, Jishnu Mukerji, Dan Nessett, Denis Pinkas, Ted Ralston, Tom Rutt, Kent Salmond, Theron Tock, and Tom Van Vleck. They are a remarkable group of professionals, and working with them and with my co-editor, Belinda Fairthorne, was a pleasure and an honor.

A number of others also contributed to the CORBAsecurity specification: Carlisle Adams, Messaoud Benantar, Nic Holt, Bill Janssen, Lynnette Khirallah, Bob Kukura, Tony Nadalin, Andrea Haessly, and Alex Thomas.

My managers at IBM, Jamil Bissar, Dave Dyar, and Jim Sides, gave me the time, the resources, and the freedom to participate in the CORBAsecurity effort. I appreciate their support and patience.

Tony Drahota, Geoff Lewis, and Andrew Watson supported the Gonville Group's work at OMG; we all appreciated their help.

Gene Jarboe has toiled ceaselessly to make sure that OMG and its members understand the importance of security; he helped pave the way for CORBAsecurity. Thanks, Gene!

Richard Herbert and Anne Hopkins went out of their way to organize, host, and chair the Gonville Group meetings. David Clarke did a lot of work to prepare the manuscript of the CORBAsecurity specification.

Konstantin Beznosov, Dave Chizmadia, Bill Herndon, and Melony Katz have chaired the OMG Security SIG, which helped to spread the CORBAsecurity gospel.

Richard Soley has been a constant supporter of CORBAsecurity. His and OMG's sponsorship of the annual DOCSEC (Distributed Object Computing SECurity) workshops is particularly appreciated.

Bret Hartman, Polar Humenn, and Jishnu Mukerji, chairs of the CORBAsecurity revision committees, have improved the CORBAsecurity specification by removing numerous small errors (and maybe one or two big ones).

My editor at Addison-Wesley, Carter Shanklin, has the patience of a saint. Pascal once wrote to a correspondent that he had made his letter longer than usual, because he lacked the time to make it short. Carter gave me the time to make this book short. I hope you appreciate it—I do.

Carter's assistant Kristin Erickson and my project editor Krysia Bebick answered all of my questions, gave me lots of helpful advice, and guided me through the editorial process with extraordinary gentleness. If you ever write a book, make sure you get editors as good as these.

My production manager, Sarah Weaver, and my copyeditor, Barbara Ames, fixed most of my stylistic quirks and were good-natured about the ones I told them not to fix. They also created the attractive layout of the book and fixed up my relatively primitive artwork. Production editors don't get a lot of credit, but they deserve a lot. Without them, you'd have to put up with ugly books full of typographical errors and unreadable sentences. The next time you see a beautiful book, remember that people like Sarah and Barbara did a lot of work to make it beautiful.

Marlena Erdos read an early draft and improved it considerably; I appreciate her thorough review very much. Her careful attention and good literary taste saved later reviewers a lot of work, and made me look like a better writer than I really am.

Matthew Hecht also read an early draft and provided thoughtful and forthright comments, which I appreciate.

Robert Vanderwall, John Weiler, Bryan Anderegg, Lydia Bennett, Richard Soley, and Jishnu Mukerji read the entire manuscript and all provided many helpful suggestions. I took almost all their advice, and will undoubtedly regret not taking the rest.

My children, Sean and Laura, endured my absence for weeks at a time over a period of several years while I worked on CORBA-security. Thanks, kids, for your understanding.

My wife, Karen, tolerated my absence and my preoccupation with CORBAsecurity and with this book. She also did something even more valuable: she read long sections of the book with a novice's eye and helped me explain lots of things more clearly. Her experience as an expert witness allowed her to spot all sorts of absurdities and mistakes in the non-repudiation chapter. Then she told me how to fix them. I'm more grateful to her than I can say.

Bob Blakley
Austin, Texas
August 1999

1

Objects and Security

What Are Objects?

This book assumes a general familiarity with object-oriented technology. If you need a good introduction, read David Taylor's book *Object-Oriented Technology: A Manager's Guide*. It's short (you can finish it in a day or two), clear, and fun to read.

If you're not familiar with object-oriented technology and you don't want to read another book before this one, here's a very quick introduction to objects (the rest of you should read along too; different books use different names for object-oriented concepts, and this quick summary will introduce you to the terms we'll use here).

Classes, objects, and messages are the building blocks of object-oriented systems

There are three kinds of things in an object-oriented system: **classes**, **objects**, and **messages**.

Classes are like recipes: They tell the system how to make objects.

Classes are recipes for objects

Objects are what you get when the system follows the recipe defined by a class. The act of creating an object using the recipe in a class is called **instantiation**, and the newly created object is called an **instance** of the class whose recipe was followed. When you follow a chocolate cake recipe's directions three times, you get three chocolate cakes. They're the same *kind* of cake, but not the *same* cake. It's just the same with classes and objects—if you instantiate the "chocolate cake" class three times, you get three chocolate cake object instances. All three objects are the same *kind* of object, but they're not the same object.

Objects are packages of procedures and data

An object contains both procedures and data. Procedures let the object *do* things; data lets the object *remember* things. Which procedures and which data an object contains is defined in its class's recipe. An object's procedures are called **methods**; its data values are called **attributes**.

Objects do work by sending messages to one another

Objects get work done by sending **messages** to other objects. Each message may ask the receiving object to do one of two things:

1. Execute one of its methods and return the result to the sender of the message.
2. Return the value of one of its attributes to the sender of the message.

How Do Objects Send Messages?

Saying "objects get work done by sending messages to other objects" glosses over a lot of real-world complexities. Objects wanting to communicate might not be running on the same machine, for example; or one object might be running, but the object it wants to send a message to might be sitting inactive on a disk.

ORBs handle the complexity of delivering messages to objects

Recognizing these complexities, an organization called the Object Management Group (OMG) saw a need for a standard service to handle chores like finding objects, waking them up, and sending messages to them. OMG called this service the Object Request Broker, or ORB, and wrote a specification describing how to build it. The specification is called the Common Object Request Broker Architecture, or CORBA.

What Is Security?

The New Merriam Webster Dictionary defines "security" as *safety,* or *freedom from worry.* Knowing this, you might guess that *computer security* should mean *safety and freedom from worry when using computers.* It would be a pretty good guess; we'll use this as our definition.

Other people (mostly security nerds like the author) sometimes define computer security in other ways. Here are a few sample definitions:

Security isn't technology; technology isn't security

- Security is confidentiality, integrity, and availability.
- Security is identification and authentication, access control, audit, and assurance.

In fact, none of this is really "security"; it's just a bunch of technology security nerds like to build. Security is what you get (maybe) if all that technology works as advertised.

What can people who sell computer equipment and software do to provide safety and freedom from worry? They could do a lot of things: They could make computers too heavy to steal (they used to, but it turns out customers like tiny, easy-to-steal computers better). They could sell insurance, so that if your computer failed or ate up all your data or e-mailed your secrets to bad guys, you'd get paid for your troubles (people are starting to do this, but it's not clear that anybody has really figured out how to do it without losing money yet). They could have a bunch of extra computers standing by, along with copies of all your important programs and data so if your computer failed, or got stolen, or got buried under millions of tons of volcanic ash, you could use theirs instead (some companies do this; they're called disaster recovery services).

The usual approach to security is protection plus assurance

Protection

The main thing the computer industry does to provide safety is called **protection**.

Protection makes you safer

Protection is usually provided by a set of *mechanisms*. Each mechanism (sometimes called a *countermeasure*) is designed to prevent a specific kind of bad thing (sometimes called a *threat*) from happening. For example, a file system access control mechanism is designed to stop people from reading and writing files they're not supposed to read and write.

The theory behind protection says that it's possible to list most of the bad things which can happen in a computer system, and it's possible to build mechanisms which can keep those things from happening.

There are three kinds of protection

There are three main kinds of protection: **authorization**, **accountability**, and **availability**.

Authorization

Authorization means no one can do things without permission

Authorization protects the system against attempts to "break the rules," as Figure 1-1 shows.

The rules generally say things like this:

- Anyone can read unclassified data.
- No one outside the company can read proprietary data.
- No one inside the company can read confidential data without first demonstrating a need to know.
- Tellers can initiate funds transfers of up to $500; managers can initiate transfers of up to $5000; transfers of over $5000 must be initiated by a vice president.
- Every account has to balance at the end of each transaction.

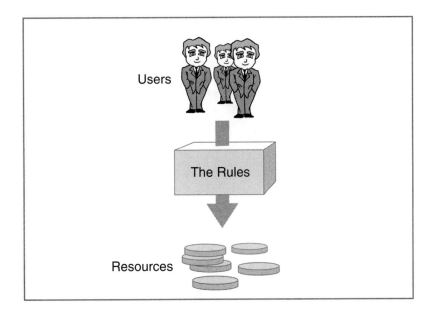

Figure 1-1
Authorization

- Every transaction has to be entered into the ledger.
- To launch the missile, two people must turn their keys at the same time.

Resources which are protected by authorization rules are called (logically enough) **protected resources**. In the preceding list above, unclassified data, proprietary data, confidential data, funds, accounts, transactions, and missiles are all protected resources.

There are lots of authorization mechanisms; most of them fall into two broad categories: access control mechanisms and data protection mechanisms.

1. *Access control* mechanisms enforce the rules. They are used in environments that can be trusted to run a program to check whether the rules are being violated as Figure 1-2 shows. In environments like this, whenever anyone asks the system for access to a protected resource, the system checks its authorization rules to see whether the access is allowed; this is called an

Authorization rules are enforced by access control and data protection mechanisms

Access control enforces the rules

5

Figure 1-2
Access control

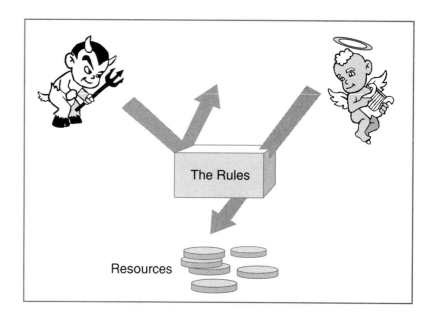

The Rules

Resources

access control check. If the rules permit the access, the system proceeds normally, but if the rules forbid the access, the system generates an error message and doesn't allow access.

2. *Data protection* mechanisms are used when the environment isn't able to run a program to check the rules or isn't trusted to enforce the rules even if it can check them.

Data protection guards data when the rules can't be enforced

A telephone wire, for example, is an environment that can't run programs, so it can't perform access control checks. A PC running DOS can run programs, but DOS isn't a secure operating system, so even if it makes an access control check, we can't be sure that a clever attacker can't bypass the check and get unauthorized access to protected resources.

Data protection is used to enforce authorization in environments like these. *Confidentiality* protection keeps unauthorized readers from snooping through protected data; *integrity* protection keeps

Figure 1-3
Data protection

vandals from making unauthorized changes to protected data. (The guy with the horns in Figure 1-3 is confused because he can't read the protected data.)

Data protection is normally implemented using encryption. The theory behind data protection is that you have to break the encryption to break the rules, and breaking the encryption is just too expensive.

Accountability

Enforcing the rules isn't always enough to keep protected resources safe. Remember, our list of sample rules included this one:

- Tellers can initiate funds transfers of up to $500; managers can initiate transfers of up to $5000; transfers of over $5000 must be initiated by a vice president.

A corrupt vice president could initiate any number of large transfers to his own account without breaking this rule!

There's no way to prevent *authorized* users with evil intent from doing things which the rules allow. And since the only rule that can keep all your protected resources safe even if your own employees turn against you is "no one is allowed to do anything," you have to take a chance and trust the people who work for you.

Accountability means you can find out who did what

The best protection available in case this trust turns out to be misplaced is called *accountability*. Accountability means you can tell who did what, when. (This is why there are footprints in Figure 1-4.)

There are two strengths of accountability: audit and non-repudiation.

Audit keeps a record of user actions

1. *Audit* is a weak form of accountability. Each user's actions are recorded in an audit log. (See Figure 1-5.) When someone suspects foul play, the audit log is examined to discover evidence of the deed and the identity of the perpetrator.

Figure 1-4
Accountability

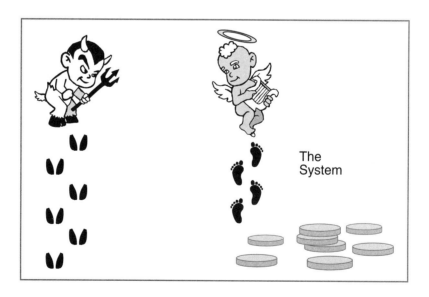

The System

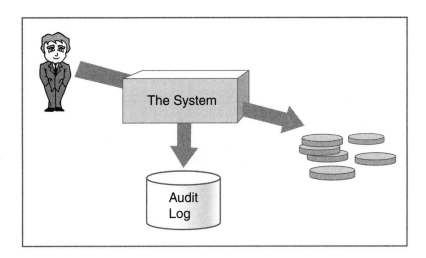

Figure 1-5 Audit

Unfortunately, some kinds of foul play can't be accurately diagnosed using audit. Privileged users may be able to impersonate other users without detection; corrupt system administrators may be able to tamper with audit logs to cover their tracks.

Because of weaknesses like these, audit log evidence may not be convincing to people who aren't owners of the system (the police, for example, or a judge and jury).

2. *Non-repudiation* protection is a stronger form of accountability. Non-repudiation protection requires users to "sign" their requests for system actions, so that their signatures can be used as evidence against them if the actions are later found to have been harmful. (See Figure 1-6.)

   Non-repudiation requires users to sign their requests

   Non-repudiation protection depends on the strength of a *digital signature* algorithm and the secrecy of each user's signature key to guarantee that privileged users and system administrators can't forge other users' signatures.

   Several governments have passed laws recognizing digital signatures as legally binding instruments under certain circumstances.

Figure 1-6
Non-repudiation

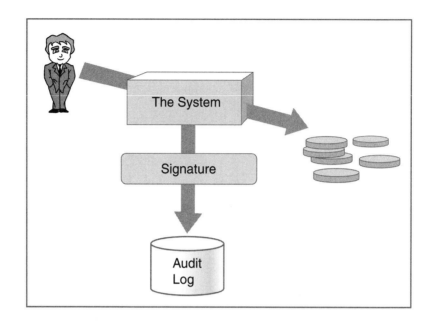

Availability

A resource is available if it's there when you need it.

A bad guy who wants to deny you the use of a resource can do various things (see Figure 1-7):

- Destroy or damage the resource
- Interfere with the communications between you and the resource (perhaps by cutting your phone line or tying up your Internet service provider's servers by sending fake packets to them)
- Interfere with your ability to pass the authorization check required for use of the resource (for example, by stealing your ATM card or by tearing up the yellow sticky note on your keyboard that had the only copy of your impossible-to-remember password written on it)

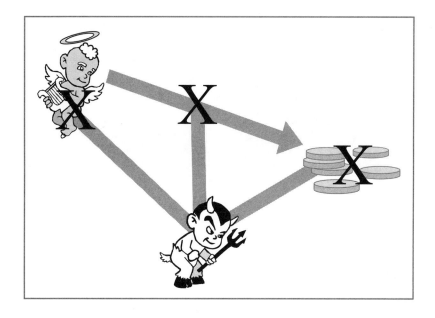

Figure 1-7
Availability

Availability protection defends you against bad guys who want to do these sorts of things. There are two approaches to availability protection: service continuity and disaster recovery.

1. *Service continuity* tries to make sure that you can always get to your resources. Service continuity protection usually involves keeping many active copies of each resource and keeping a couple of independent communication paths open to each copy. (See Figure 1-8.)

2. *Disaster recovery* assumes that service will eventually be interrupted, and it figures out how you can get back up and running after the interruption.

   Disaster recovery protection usually consists of keeping backup copies of everything (including cryptographic keys and hardware) and planning in advance how the backups will be activated and used in an emergency. (See Figure 1-9.)

Service continuity keeps the system up and running

Disaster recovery builds a spare system for a rainy day

Figure 1-8
Service continuity

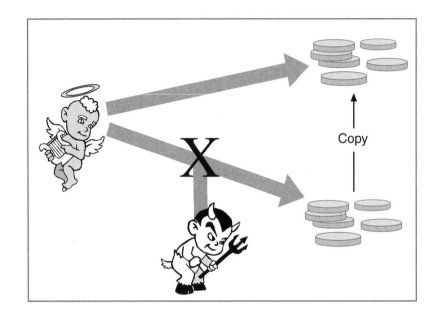

Copy

Figure 1-9
Disaster recovery

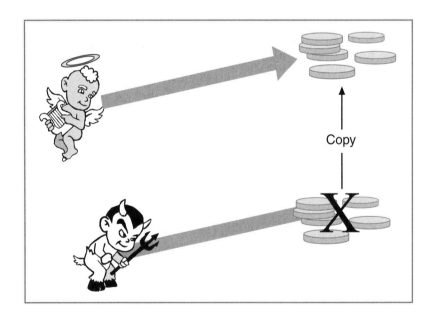

Copy

Assurance

What the computer industry does to provide freedom from worry is called *assurance*. Assurance is the set of things the builder and the operator of a system do to convince you that it really is safe to use.

The theory behind assurance is that the computer industry knows what things need to be done to make a system secure, can convince you that doing those things will make the system secure, and can prove that those things have been done for your particular system.

Assurance relieves worry

If you care about security, someone who wants to sell you a secure system or who wants to convince you to use a supposedly secure system has to convince you that

Assurance means the system keeps its security promises

- the system can enforce the policy you're interested in, and
- the system works.

If you think the system won't support your policy, the seller or operator can simply bring up the system's policy management interface, ask you what your policy is, and try to enter it into the system. If he succeeds, he wins—you're convinced. If not, he loses—no sale.

If you think the system doesn't work, the seller or operator has to convince you that the system keeps its security promises. To do this, he has to make an *assurance argument*.

Assurance arguments usually try to prove three things:

1. The system's protection mechanisms are correct (in other words, they're not full of bugs, and they enforce the stated policy).
2. The system always uses its protection mechanisms when they're needed (for example, it always checks access control whenever a user asks for access to a protected resource).

3. There's no way to circumvent the system's protection mechanisms (so the system doesn't have any "back doors" which might let people do end-runs around the protection mechanisms).

Assurance has to be done throughout the system's lifetime

Winning the assurance argument involves showing that the system has been designed, built, delivered, installed, and configured properly, and that it is being operated properly.

Three kinds of *assurance activities* contribute to a strong assurance argument:

Design assurance ensures that a secure system is designed

1. *Design assurance* consists of using good security engineering practices to identify important threats and to choose appropriate countermeasures.

Development assurance ensures that the designed system gets built

2. *Development assurance* requires the use of disciplined processes to implement the design correctly and to deliver the implemented system securely and reliably to the customer.
3. *Operational assurance* mandates secure installation, configuration, and day-to-day operation of the system.

Operational assurance ensures that the system is used securely

Assurance activities are necessary but not sufficient for a good assurance argument; there must also be *evidence* to prove that the activities were performed.

Assurance evidence lets you see what assurance was done

Good records must be kept during every phase of a system's life (design, development, distribution, installation, and operation) so that people who want to evaluate the system can figure out what has been done to make it secure and decide how much faith in the system's security is justified.

2

Object Security

Object-oriented systems, like other systems, address the security requirements (authorization, accountability, and availability) by applying protection based on policy. In a little more detail, object security

Object security is like security in other environments . . .

- Prevents unauthorized use of objects by enforcing access control based on a set of authorization policy rules
- Generates and records evidence to ensure that users can be held accountable for their use of objects
- Ensures that objects are available when authorized users need to use them

While securing an object-oriented system is similar in general to securing other kinds of systems, some of the details differ because object-oriented systems present special security challenges.

. . . but not exactly like security in other environments

Object-oriented systems tend not to have rigid naming hierarchies. This means that there are more objects with aliases, and more anonymous objects, than many policy administrators are used to.

Scale, naming, and encapsulation are special problems

Object-oriented systems often have more objects, and more types of objects, than procedural systems. This complicates the policy administrator's job because there are more things to apply policies to.

Finally, objects mix code and data and blur the distinction between them by hiding them both behind the veil of encapsulation. This obscures exactly which resources can be reached through each object's interface—and so makes it harder for the security administrator to assess risks and set policy.

The next section lists some specific things a security system needs to do to deal with the special problems of naming, scale, and encapsulation which arise in the object-oriented environment.

Special Object Security Requirements

Naming, scale, and encapsulation cause problems in object-oriented systems which don't arise in other kinds of systems.

Naming

Most of the securable objects in procedural systems have unique names or identifiers. Almost all the objects in object-oriented systems are securable, but a lot of them have no names, and even more have no unique names. This makes stating security policies hard, because it's tough to tell the system to protect a thing without using the thing's name.

ORBs locate objects using references

In the Preface we said that object-oriented systems call the act of creating a new object "instantiation" because each newly created object is an "instance" of the class which defines its methods and attributes.

When a user (or program) asks an object-oriented system to instantiate a class, the system uses information in the class's definition to set aside a chunk of memory which will contain the new object's code and data and to write some information into that memory (this is called "initializing" the object).

When the system is done with instantiating the new object, the system's ORB makes up a **reference** which it can use to find the chunk of memory containing the object's code and data the next time somebody wants to send a message to the object.

In most object-oriented systems, this reference is just a number (like `0x1013AE28`). Within the specific copy of the specific ORB that created the reference, an object's reference is unique to that object for as long as it exists, but there's no guarantee that another ORB, or another copy of the same ORB, won't use the same number for a different object. There's also no guarantee that the same ORB won't reuse the number later, after the object has been disposed of, to refer to a different object. So the reference isn't really useful as a name for the object.

References are not names

Many object-oriented systems provide "naming services." A naming service allows a user or program to attach a name to an object as a property. Naming services also allow users and programs to translate back and forth between names and references. Naming services don't usually allow the same name to be used to refer to different objects.

Objects can have names . . .

But most naming services allow the same object to have more than one name. And no naming service can prevent the system from creating objects that don't have names at all.

. . . but some objects have many names, and many have none at all

Since some objects don't have the "name" property, object-oriented security systems need to tie security policy to some other property which all objects, or at least all objects that need to be secured, are guaranteed to have. Unfortunately, the only property which *all* objects are guaranteed to have is a reference, and references are very hard to read and understand. A screenful of policies based on object references might look like this:

How do administrators refer to objects when stating policy?

```
0x01A3F5EE : Dept_563 may (READ), Admin may (WRITE)
0x1AA44709 : Admin may (READ and WRITE)
0x55F53001 : VPs may (READ and WRITE), Admin may (READ)
```

Security administrators are going to have a lot of trouble remembering what the references (the numbers in the left-hand column) mean.

We could make the system assign a name to all objects that need to be secured, but as the next section will explain, this would cause other problems. What's really needed is a new property which every securable object will have, and which will be a good basis for managing security policies.

Requirement: Object-oriented security systems should let security administrators define an object's policy without having to know its name. Objects with no names should be securable; objects with many names should be securable and should be secured by the same policy no matter which name is used to refer to them.

Scale

Compared to procedural systems, object-oriented systems have too many objects and too many types of objects.

There are too many objects

A typical object-oriented system has at least tens of thousands of objects; some systems may even have many millions. It isn't reasonable to expect a security administrator to define tens of thousands of rules, let alone millions. It's also expensive to store that many rules and to look through them while the system is running to find which ones apply to a user's request.

Policy should apply to groups of objects

A good security system would let administrators assign a single policy to any *group* of objects whose members have similar protection needs.

Procedural systems often create security policy groups using the naming hierarchy. File systems, for example, let security administrators assign an access control policy to a directory and then apply that policy to all the files in the directory.

This really isn't a very good system. Naming hierarchies are designed to make it easy to *find* things; people tend to choose names which describe the contents of the things named. Groups (like directories) in naming hierarchies therefore tend to contain things with similar contents.

Policy groups shouldn't be based on resource names

To make it easy to *protect* things, you need to group them based on sensitivity or value.

It would be perfectly natural for a CIA analyst to create a directory at the beginning of a new project and, over time, put all the files related to that project into it. Figure 2-1 is an example of what such a directory might look like.

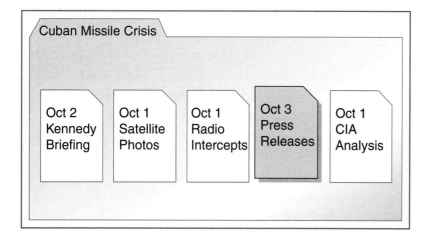

Figure 2-1 Similar names with different policies

Cuban Missile Crisis				
Oct 2 Kennedy Briefing	Oct 1 Satellite Photos	Oct 1 Radio Intercepts	Oct 3 Press Releases	Oct 1 CIA Analysis

Even though these files all "belong" in the same directory based on their relationship to the Cuban missile crisis project, it's pretty clear that it wouldn't be a good idea to assign them all the same access control policy. The press releases should surely be *unclassified*; everything else is likely *top secret*. Here's what's needed:

Requirement: *Object-oriented security systems should let security administrators assign objects to* policy groups. *Security policies should be assigned to policy groups, not to individual objects. A policy group's security policy should apply to all its members. Objects should not be required to have similar names in order to belong to the same policy group. Objects with similar names should not be required to belong to the same policy group.*

Procedural systems have few system resource types and few operations

Procedural systems define a small number of types of system resources (for example, directories, files, and databases). Normally it's not possible (for anyone except the system vendor) to extend the set of system resources a procedural system supports. Each type of system resource can be manipulated using a small set of system-defined operations (for example, for files, "read," "write," "execute," "create," and "delete"). Procedural programs use the system-defined operations to get at the data inside system resources, and then they do all the complicated work in their own code. The system sees only the simple system-defined data-access operations; all the complicated work of data transformation is hidden from view because it happens inside program code which doesn't perform any system calls. Figure 2-2 shows a procedural program using system-defined operations to access protected system resources. It also shows a direct access, bypassing system security, to the data inside a protected system resource, and direct access to unprotected, non-system resources.

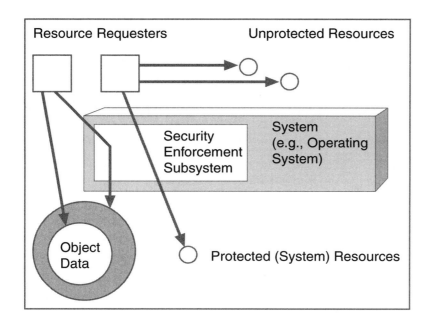

Figure 2-2
Security in a
procedural system

Object-oriented systems wrap code and data up inside each object. They allow programmers to create a very large number of different types of objects by defining new classes. Each class provides customized functions, accessible through a set of operations specific to the class. Because all operations are invoked using messages, which are transmitted and dispatched by the system, the system can see both data-access and data-transformation requests. Nothing is hidden from the system except the algorithms which implement individual operations. Figure 2-3 shows that in an object-oriented system, all resources can be protected because all resource requests go through the ORB as messages.

Object-oriented systems have many classes and many operations

We've just seen three important differences between object-oriented and procedural systems:

1. Object-oriented system code sees *messages*; procedural system code sees *system calls*.

Figure 2-3 Security
in an object-
oriented system

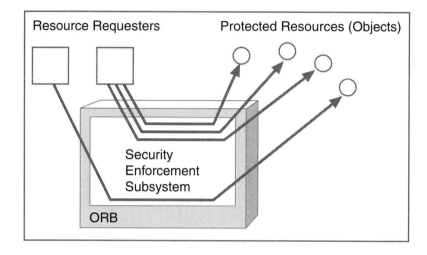

Resource Requesters   Protected Resources (Objects)

Security
Enforcement
Subsystem

ORB

2. All operations on all objects in an object-oriented system are
   invoked using messages; in a procedural system only *data-access
   operations* on *system objects* are invoked using system calls.
3. In an object-oriented system, application programmers *can*
   create new classes of objects; in a procedural system, they usually *cannot* create new types of system resources.

From a security point of view, these differences add up to good
news and bad news.

First, the good news: An object-oriented system's security policy
can be very specific about what can be done to the system's objects
because it sees many more types of operations than a procedural
system does.

Now the bad news: Controlling the use of lots of types of operations
is complicated because a security administrator has to understand
each type of operation and figure out who should be allowed to
use it.

Security systems for object-oriented environments should aim to keep the good news and get rid of the bad news:

Requirement: Object-oriented security systems should let security administrators control access to individual methods of an object. However, administrators should not need to understand what every method in the system does in order to administer policy. The system should let administrators apply a single policy to all methods with similar functionality or sensitivity.

Encapsulation

Most protected resources in procedural systems are passive; they consist only of data which is read or written by programs that access them. (There are exceptions, like stored procedures in relational databases, but they are exceptions, and the security policies of procedural systems don't provide administrators with very granular or flexible control over their use.)

In object-oriented systems, essentially all protected resources (that is, objects) are at least potentially active: They contain code as well as data, and that code may do complicated things underneath a seemingly simple interface. What's more, because of "encapsulation" (the property of objects that you can't look inside them to see what they contain), neither an object's clients nor its security administrators can tell how much complexity is lurking under that interface. For the object's clients, this is good news. It means they don't need to deal with, or even know about, how an object does the work they ask for through the object's interface.

Encapsulation hides objects' internals . . .

For security administrators, the news isn't so good. Encapsulation hides important information about the structure of the system. Without this information, it's very hard to figure out what policy is needed to protect the system.

. . . but security administrators need to know about objects' internals

To see why, imagine that your grandmother has a safe-deposit box at her bank. Let's say she keeps her secret recipe for cheesecake (worth a million dollars!) in it. Obviously, grandma wants to keep the recipe secure; that's why she has the safe-deposit box. As long as the recipe is in the box, only grandma can get it out, because only she has the key to the box.

Now imagine that the recipe is in a computer file and the safe-deposit box is an object. As long as the recipe is inside the object as data, and the object system enforces an access control policy which keeps everyone but grandma from looking at it, the recipe is still secure.

But what if the recipe is itself an object? Things get a lot trickier. Remember we said that objects are represented by references? So if the recipe is an object, what's really inside the safe-deposit box object is not the recipe object itself but a reference to it. In the real world, this would be like grandma burying the recipe in the back-yard and putting a map of the backyard with a big "X" on it into the safe-deposit box, as in Figure 2-4.

Putting a treasure map in the box isn't as good as putting the recipe in the box, for two reasons:

1. There might be other copies of the map.
2. People might be able to find the recipe without using the map (by digging up the whole backyard, for example).

In either case, no amount of access control on the safe-deposit box object is going to keep the recipe secure.

An Overview of the CORBAsecurity Model

This chapter has concentrated on the object security *problem*. The rest of the book will describe OMG's *solution*—CORBAsecurity—in detail. Before you dive into that detail, this section gives you a

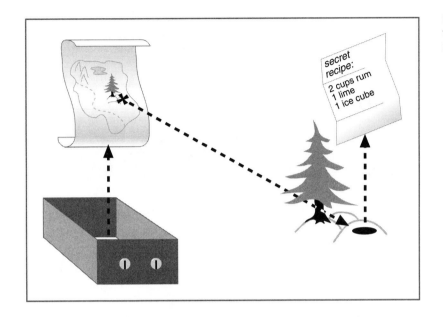

Figure 2-4 The
treasure-map
problem

quick overview of the CORBAsecurity model so you can have the big picture in the back of your mind as you read.

CORBA systems address security requirements by applying protection based on policy. In a CORBA system, a policy applies to a *domain*.

Administrators manage policy using domains

Administrators can apply policy to an object by putting the object into a domain and setting up policy for the domain. Figure 2-5 shows this.

Chapter 3 tells you more about policy.

When you start up an ORB, it creates a new **execution context** for you. This execution context stores a bunch of information the ORB needs to have in order to keep track of your use of the ORB.

User information is stored in execution contexts

Figure 2-5 Policy
applied to a domain

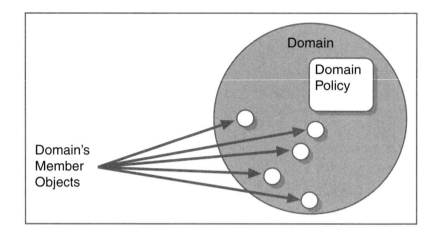

*Credentials define
user identity and
privileges*

Part of the information the ORB stores in your execution context is
a **credential**, which describes your identity and privileges. When
the ORB doesn't know anything about you (because you haven't
logged on yet, for example), the ORB assigns a default credential.

Chapter 4 covers the details of execution contexts, credentials, and
authentication.

*The ORB enforces
policy*

Once the user has established a credential and the administrator
has set up the system's policy, the ORB can do most of the rest of
the heavy lifting. The ORB enforces most security policies transparently—without the knowledge of the objects which are being protected and the applications which are calling those objects. Most
programs in a secure ORB don't need to be aware of security at all.

The ORB always knows what execution context is active, so it
always knows whose credentials to use when making policy decisions. The ORB also knows how to find out what domain any object
belongs to, so it can find the policies that need to be enforced
whenever a message is sent to any object. Finally, of course, the

ORB sees all the messages that get sent, so it can always check to see if a message conforms to the system's policy and refuse to send the message if it doesn't conform. Figure 2-6 illustrates how the ORBs enforce policy.

The ORB enforces access control, message protection, and audit policies transparently. Chapter 5 explains how the ORB enforces access control; Chapter 6 explains how the ORB protects the confidentiality and integrity of messages; and Chapter 8 explains how the ORB audits security-sensitive operations.

Although CORBA client applications and the objects they call don't need to know about security to get the benefit of the protection the ORB provides, the ORB exposes its security functions through a callable interface. This lets CORBA applications call the security services if they want to customize the protection the system provides.

Objects which really need to deal with security, can

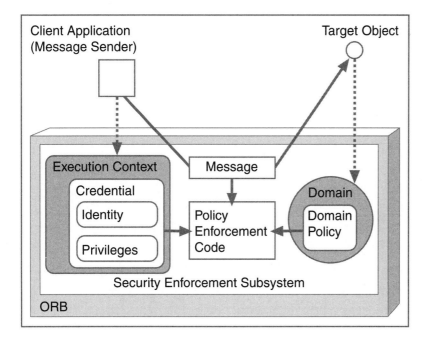

Figure 2-6 How ORBs enforce policy

For example, objects which aren't satisfied with the access control policy enforced by the ORB can use the security interface to define and enforce their own access control policies.

The ORB's security interface also allows the system to support security policies that require user interaction. Many non-repudiation policies require the user to take an explicit positive action to apply a digital signature (so that the system can't digitally sign things behind the user's back). Chapter 9 explains how the non-repudiation service works and why the ORB does not enforce non-repudiation protection transparently.

3

Policy

Protection and Policy

Policy describes which user actions are allowed and which are forbidden. Policy may also describe actions which the system itself must perform, and when it must perform them.

Protection is based on policy

Policy is expressed using policy rules. Here's a very simple policy rule:

Policy rules define policy

> *Anyone may read unclassified files.*

Reading policy rules is a lot like diagramming sentences (remember fifth-grade English?). The policy rule above is a complete sentence, with a subject, a verb, and an object.

subject: anyone

verb: (may) read

object: unclassified files

Security terminology isn't exactly the same as the terminology of English grammar, but it's very close. The "subject" of a policy rule, which defines *who* the rule applies to, is called a "subject." The "verb" of a policy rule, which describes *what* the subject is allowed to do, is called an "action." And the "object" of a policy rule, which describes *which* things the subject is allowed to act upon, is called an "object." So the policy above has the following elements:

The elements of policy are subjects, objects, and actions

subject: anyone

action: (may) read

object: unclassified files

More complicated policy rules are possible; in particular, it's sometimes useful to be able to state *conditional* policies like the following:

> *Between 8 A.M. and 5 P.M. on business days, Fred may execute*
> *financial transactions under $1000.*

Conditional policies have one extra element, called (logically) the *condition*. If the condition is true, then the policy is enforced; otherwise, it is not. The elements of our example conditional policy are:

condition: Between 8 A.M. and 5 P.M. business days

subject: Fred

action: (may) execute

object: financial transactions under $1000

The general form of a policy rule is:

if

condition

then

subject (may, must, may not, *or* must not) do **action** to
object

Policy rules which are always in force (that is, rules which aren't really conditional) can still be written using this general form, by specifying "true" as the condition.

Subjects

Subjects are the active entities in a system; they ask the system to do work or to reveal or update information. CORBA systems identify subjects using *credentials*. The next chapter will describe subjects and credentials in more detail.

Objects

In object-oriented environments, the "objects" in policy rules are just that—objects (that is, instances of classes).

Actions

The actions in an object-oriented system's policy rules are method invocations.

In Chapter 5 we'll see an example of controlling access to printer objects. In that example, the system's policy contains the following rule, which allows a subject named Joe to invoke a method called **submit_job:**

> Joe may do **submit_job** to laser1.

In an object-oriented environment, all data and transactions flow through the object messaging infrastructure: The ORB passes clients' requests to target objects and passes the responses back. Because the ORB handles all traffic, it can look at each request or response and see whether it's legal according to the security policy rules. This means that the ORB can enforce the system's security policy even if all clients and target objects are completely security-unaware. In other words, the security provided by the ORB is "transparent" to clients and applications, as Figure 3-1 shows.

In object environments, actions are method invocations

The ORB enforces policy transparently

Figure 3-1 ORBs
apply policy to all
messages

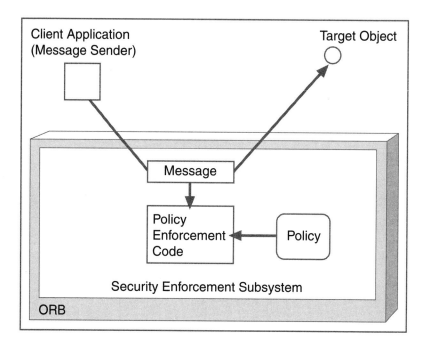

Object-oriented systems can (and must) enforce many kinds of
policy. CORBA ORBs which implement the CORBAsecurity services
currently support enforcement of four kinds of policies: access control, audit, data protection, and non-repudiation.

Access Control Policy

Access control policies control which subjects can invoke operations
on objects in the system. The general form of an access control policy rule is

subject may do **invoke method** to **object**

Message Protection Policy

Message protection policy specifies how messages from client programs to target objects are protected. The general form of a message protection policy is

ORB must do **apply specified QOP** to **message**

QOP in this rule means **Quality of Protection**; CORBAsecurity supports three quality of protection options:

Authentication requires one or more parties to prove their identities. CORBAsecurity allows data protection policy to require the message's originator, its receiver, or both to prove their identities.

Integrity requires the message to be protected against modification.

Confidentiality requires the message to be protected against disclosure.

Audit Policy

There are three broad classes of audit policies:

1. Event generation policies control when the system generates audit event records in response to user-initiated or system-initiated events. The general form of an event generation policy is

    if

    action matches pattern

    then

    system must do **generate** to **new audit event**

2. Event disposition policies govern what the system does with audit events after they're generated. The general form of an event disposition policy is

> if
>
> > **audit event matches pattern**
>
> then
>
> > **audit subsystem** must do (**log** *or* **raise alert** or **discard**) to **audit event**

3. Audit service continuity policies govern what the system does when the audit subsystem can't function as required. The general form of an audit service continuity policy is

> if
>
> > (**audit log full** *or* **audit service unavailable**)
>
> then
>
> > **system** must do (**halt** *or* **raise alert and continue**)

CORBAsecurity supports event generation and event disposition policies but not audit service continuity policies.

Non-Repudiation Policy

Non-repudiation provides evidence (like a signature or a receipt) that a particular subject performed some action on some object.

Non-repudiation policy defines the rules for generating and verifying non-repudiation evidence.

Non-repudiation evidence generation policy tells the system under what circumstances non-repudiation evidence should be generated, whose signature(s) need to be applied to the evidence, and who needs to be able to verify the evidence's validity. The general format of non-repudiation evidence generation policy is

if

action matches pattern

then

subject initiating action must do **generate** to **new**

non-repudiation evidence

Non-repudiation evidence verification policy tells the system under what circumstances non-repudiation evidence must be provided, whose signature(s) are acceptable on the evidence, and what has to be done to verify the evidence's validity. The general form of non-repudiation evidence verification policy is:

if

action matches pattern

then

subject receiving request must do **verify** to **non-repudiation evidence**

4

Identification, Authentication, and Privilege

Before an object system can safely allow a subject to use its resources, it needs to know who the subject is.

The CORBAsecurity model divides the system's process of discovering who the user is into three steps: First, the system asks the subject to **identify** itself. Then, because the subject might be lying in order to get unauthorized access, it **authenticates** the subject's claimed identity. Finally, after it's satisfied that the subject's identity is authentic, it checks to see if the subject has any special **privileges**.

Subjects

A *subject* is anything that tries to use a computer system or its resources. Each subject is presumed to have an *independent will*—this independence of will is what makes it a subject and distinguishes it from every other subject. Whenever the system is asked to do something, it assumes that the request represents the *will* of some subject. Before it agrees to the request, the system tries to identify which subject made the request.

The most familiar subjects are people, but nonhuman subjects exist, too. Programs can be subjects when they're doing things without

There are many kinds of subjects

specific commands from users. Hardware devices can be subjects. If you could train a gorilla to use a computer, it would be a subject.

Subjects are outside the system's control

A subject, by definition, has an independent will. So the system can't control what a subject does; it can only control whether it will do what the subject asks it to do. Policy defines what the system will do for each subject. To enforce policy, the system has to be able to tell the difference between subjects and to make judgments about them. To do this, the system has to be able to describe subjects' security-relevant properties.

Security attributes describe subjects

Security attributes are the "adjectives" a CORBA system uses to describe subjects' security-relevant properties. The system might describe a particular subject this way:

> the subject is
>
> > named **Josephine Bonaparte**
> >
> > **Empress of the French**
> >
> > cleared to see **Secret** information
> >
> > a member of the **Royalty**

Security attributes are either identities or privileges

There are two basic types of subject security attributes: *identities*, which apply to a single subject, and *privilege attributes*, which may be shared by many subjects.

Identities describe unique properties of a subject

Identities are used to describe properties of a subject which are unique; they distinguish the subject from all other subjects. The traditional "username" is an example of an identity; CORBA systems call this kind of subject security attribute an *access identity*. In our example, the subject's access identity would be **Josephine Bonaparte**. Subjects can have more than one unique characteristic, so they can have more than one identity (for example, a driver's license number is an identity, but you don't have to choose between having a driver's license number and having a name).

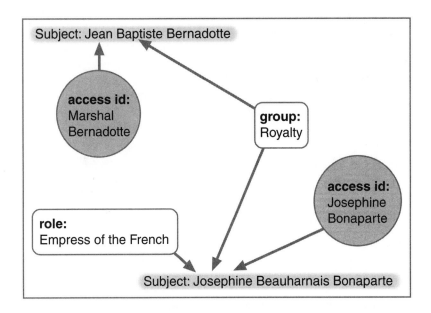

Figure 4-1 Subjects
and their security
attributes

Privilege attributes are used to describe properties of a subject
which may also apply to other subjects. Examples of privilege
attributes include *groups*, *roles*, and *clearances*. In our example, the
subject has the role **Empress of the French**, belongs to the group
Royalty, and holds **Secret** clearance.

*Privilege attributes
may be shared
among subjects*

Figure 4-1 illustrates the relationships between subjects and their
subject security attributes; in the figure, identities are represented
by circles and privilege attributes are represented by rounded
rectangles.

Figure 4-1 shows that a single subject may have many subject security attributes (Josephine has three attributes: the access identity
"Josephine Bonaparte," the role "Empress of the French," and the
group "Royalty"). The security system may need to use several of

*Credentials are
collections of subject
security attributes*

Figure 4-2
Credentials are
containers for
security attributes

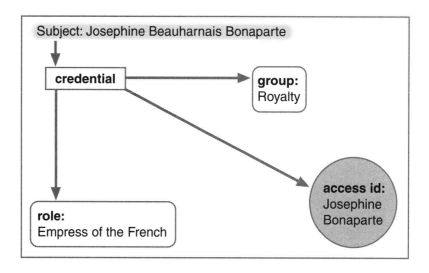

these attributes, or all of them, when it makes policy decisions. To
keep track of a subject's security attributes, the system collects them
into a **credential**, as Figure 4-2 illustrates.

Authentication and Credentials

*Subjects' identities
are unknown at first*

When the system encounters a new subject (for example, when a
user walks up to one of the system's terminals or when a new program starts to run), it assigns the subject a default credential.

*Unidentified subjects
are assigned a
default public
credential*

The initial default credential the system assigns to a new subject
contains no identities and only one privilege attribute, called
"public." (See Figure 4-3.) This credential tells the system that it
doesn't yet know which subject it's dealing with; the subject could
be anyone in the general public.

Subjects with only the public security attribute may be allowed to
use the system for some limited purposes (reading publicly available information, for example). And some subjects may be content

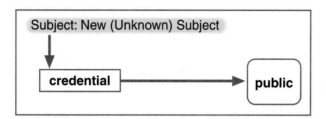

Figure 4-3
Everyone gets
the public
security attribute

with this level of access: They may never need to use any security attributes other than "public."

Many subjects will need to do things the system won't let the general public do, though. These subjects will need to claim more powerful security attributes.

Many operations require nonpublic security attributes

The way a subject claims nonpublic security attributes is by *authenticating* itself. CORBA systems provide an object which authenticates subjects; it's called a *PrincipalAuthenticator*. Subjects authenticate themselves by identifying themselves (telling the PrincipalAuthenticator their names) and supplying some *authentication data* (like a password, a mother's maiden name, or a fingerprint scan). The PrincipalAuthenticator looks over the authentication data; If it's satisfied that the subject is who (or what) it claims to be, it builds a credential with an appropriate set of security attributes and hands it back, as Figure 4-4 shows.

Subjects get nonpublic security attributes through authentication

It's important to realize that some kinds of authentication data don't work well with some kinds of subjects. Take fingerprint scans, for example. Programs don't have fingers, and fingerprint scanners probably aren't tuned correctly for gorilla fingers, so if you have a lot of programmatic or gorilla subjects in your system, you might want to go with some other kind of authentication technology.

41

Figure 4-4 Principal-
Authentication

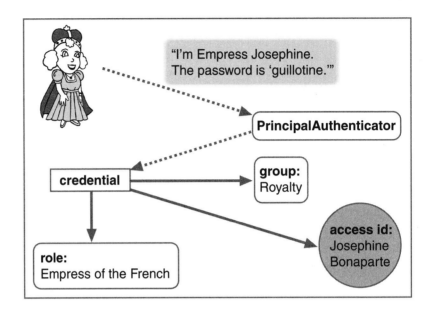

Contexts

After a subject has been authenticated and given a credential, the system needs to put the credential somewhere (so that it can remember who the subject is) and associate it with the subject's later actions. The place the system keeps a subject's credentials is called an **execution context**.

The system stores credentials in execution contexts

An execution context is the collection of information the system uses to keep track of the work it's doing. For example, the system needs some context information to remember which actions have been completed and which are still being worked on (some systems even keep enough context information to allow them to *undo* actions after they've been completed).

From a security point of view, one interesting part of the execution context is the information that's used to figure out who's responsible for requests and actions.

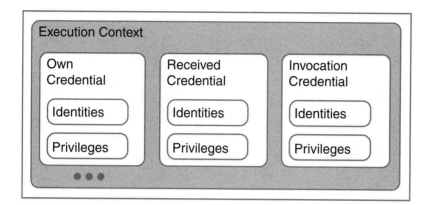

Figure 4-5
Execution context

CORBA execution contexts keep track of subject identity information by storing credential objects. Each execution context stores three credentials, as Figure 4-5 shows.

Each execution context holds three types of credentials

The **own credential** identifies the subject under whose authority the context is executing.

The **received credential** identifies the subject from whom the execution context has most recently received a message (this may be null if the execution context doesn't contain code capable of receiving messages or hasn't yet received any).

The **invocation credential** represents the subject identity the execution context will use the next time it sends a message. Normally this will be the same as the own credential, but as we'll see in Chapter 7, if the execution context has become a delegate for someone from whom it's received a message, the invocation credential may be the same as the received credential.

CORBA systems provide an object, called **Current**, which represents the active execution context. A program can find out what execution context it's in and what that context's credentials are by calling the ORB to get its Current object and then querying Current

The Current object represents the active execution context

**Figure 4-6 Each
execution context
belongs to a domain**

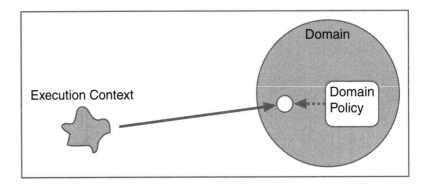

to discover any of the credentials associated with the current execution context.

*Some security policies
apply to the whole
system*

Some security policies aren't associated with specific objects. For example, policies that say

> *every message sent from this system must be encrypted*

or

> *no one can access pornographic pictures from this system*

apply to the system rather than to any specific object in it.

*Execution contexts
belong to domains*

To support policies like these, CORBA systems allow the ORB to assign execution contexts to domains, as Figure 4-6 shows.

Whenever a program running in an execution context sends or receives a message, the ORB enforces the policies associated with the context's domain. For example, if the context's domain contains a message protection policy (see Chapter 6) requiring that messages be encrypted, the ORB encrypts the message before sending it. If the context's domain contains an access control policy that prohibits sending messages to the designated target, the ORB refuses to send the message. Or if the context's domain contains an audit policy that requires auditing of the message, the ORB generates an audit event.

5

Access Control

An object system's access control policy determines which subjects can use each object's methods. This prevents unauthorized subjects from using information inside objects.

For access control to work properly, an object security system must give security administrators a way to create and manage policies, and it must give the ORB a way to enforce policies when subjects ask to invoke methods on objects. The CORBAsecurity model does both.

Access control protects information inside objects

Managing Access Control Policy

Security policy management models which aren't carefully designed to keep the number of rules under control can break down when the systems they protect get big. CORBAsecurity provides a policy management model that allows administrators to define very detailed policies for very big systems using just a few policy rules.

The Problem of Scale

The worst problem with access control policy, especially in object systems, is that there's so much of it. Remember we said in Chapter 3 that the general form of an access control policy rule is

Access control policy scales poorly

subject may do **invoke method** to **object**

This rule names a subject, a method, and an object.

In a system with 100 subjects, and 1000 objects with 10 methods each, an administrator who wants to control every possible access needs to write a lot of rules.

Look at Figure 5-1. Big boxes represent objects, little boxes represent methods, and arrows represent access control policy rules. Since there are 1000 objects with 10 methods each, the administrator has had to write 10,000 rules just to describe what the first subject can and can't do. To complete the policy, the administrator will have to write 10,000 rules for each of the system's 100 subjects—for a total of 1,000,000 rules.

This obviously isn't going to work, even for fairly small systems. What's needed is some way to reduce the number of rules the administrator has to write.

Figure 5-1 Way too much access control policy

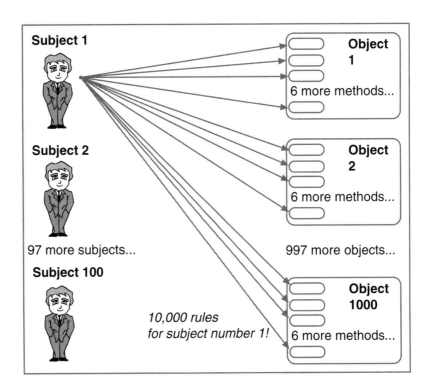

Controlling Access Control Policy Scale

CORBAsecurity gives security administrators three tools to control the scale of access control policy: privilege attributes, domains, and required rights.

Privilege Attributes Are Groups of Subjects

We talked about privilege attributes in Chapter 4. Privilege attributes allow administrators to lump subjects together in bunches; this helps to keep the amount of policy data under control by letting administrators apply the same policy to a bunch of subjects without having to write a new (identical) rule for each subject. Of course, this only works if there are subjects in the system who should have the same access—but this is true in most systems.

Figure 5-2 shows what happens when we allow administrators to use privilege attributes in policy rules. There are still 1000 objects with 10 methods each, and there are still 100 subjects, but the subjects have now been divided into two bunches, each one represented by a privilege attribute (**VPs** and **engineers**). So now, instead of 100 sets of 10,000 rules, there are only two sets of 10,000 rules (one set for VPs and one set for engineers). This leaves us with 20,000 rules in all—an 80% reduction! It's a great start, but there are still way too many rules.

Privilege attributes reduce the number of subjects for which rules need to be defined

In real-world systems, of course, it won't usually be possible to divide all subjects neatly into just *two* bunches. But it will usually be possible to divide all the subjects in a normal system into a small number of bunches, each represented by a privilege attribute.

You may be wondering why I've used the strange word "bunches" here, instead of a more common word like "groups." It's because there are different kinds of "bunches" which make sense in different environments. Sometimes the right kind of "bunch" really is a "group"—just an arbitrary collection of subjects. Sometimes it's a "role"—a collection of subjects who perform the same job function. Sometimes it's a "clearance"—a collection of subjects with the same

Different types of privilege attributes describe different kinds of groups of subjects

47

Figure 5-2 Less
access control
policy, but still too
much

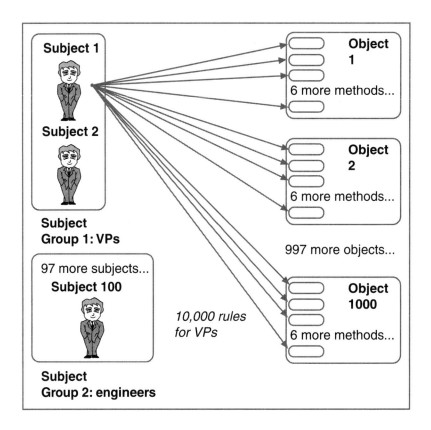

kind of need-to-know rights to see sensitive information. The
CORBAsecurity model defines a privilege attribute type for each of
these kinds of "bunch," and security administrators can use any of
these privilege attribute types—or all of them—at the same time.

Domains Are Groups of Objects

We introduced domains in Chapter 2. Figure 5-3 should look familiar.

Domains reduce the
number of objects for
which rules need to
be defined

A **domain** is a collection of objects plus a set of policies. Each
domain has at most one access control policy. This policy controls
access to all of the objects which are members of the domain—no
matter how many members the domain has. Let's look at our
example again; in Figure 5-4, we've grouped all the objects in our
system into 10 domains.

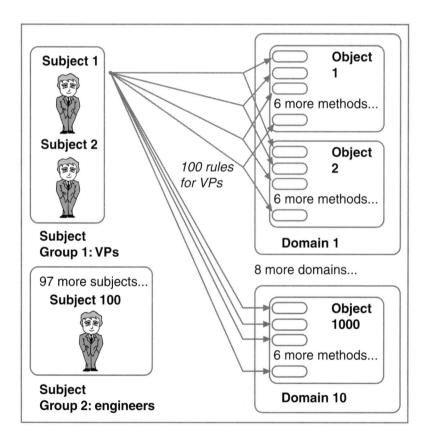

Figure 5-3 A domain

Domain

Domain Policy

Domain's Member Objects

Figure 5-4 Just a little too much access control policy

Subject 1

Subject 2

Subject Group 1: VPs

97 more subjects...
Subject 100

Subject Group 2: engineers

100 rules for VPs

Object 1

6 more methods...

Object 2

6 more methods...

Domain 1

8 more domains...

Object 1000

6 more methods...

Domain 10

Now we only need 10 rules for each domain. Each rule will control access to one method of *all* the objects in a domain. (OK, I'm cheating. I'm assuming that all the objects in each domain have exactly the same 10 methods. This isn't really true most of the time, but we'll talk about how to deal with that problem in the next section.) Since there are only 10 domains, this means we are down to 100 rules per subject, or a total of 200 rules, since we've only got two subjects. This is another huge improvement, and we're getting close to a manageable number of rules.

Required Rights Are Groups of Actions

Remember that an object's actions are invoked using *methods*. Because an object could support any number of actions, and because those actions could have very different consequences, it's important for security administrators to be able to restrict access to individual methods (not just to whole objects).

Security administrators need to be able to control access to individual methods (not just to whole objects)

To see why, imagine that your system had an object representing your e-mail inbox. Clearly this object needs to have at least two methods, one to put an e-mail message into the inbox, and another to get an e-mail message out of the inbox. You probably want lots of people to be able to use the **put** method, but you don't want anyone other than yourself to be able to use the **get** method. No access rule that applies to the whole inbox object will support this policy; each method needs its own rule:

> **I** may do **get** to **inbox**
>
> **anyone** may do **put** to **inbox**

But managing policy for individual methods causes three problems

But creating rules for each method in an object-oriented system would cause three problems for security administrators.

The first problem is the number of different methods. A typical class has about 10 methods, so a typical system has about ten times as many methods as classes. In large systems this means that the security administrator has to learn (and remember) the meanings of a lot of methods—maybe hundreds or even thousands of them.

First, there are too many methods

The second problem is that methods which do similar or even identical things may have different names. This means that administrators have to say the same thing several times in several different ways when they administer access control rules.

Second, similar methods may have different names

Figure 5-5 shows a system with two classes of printer objects. See the "submit_job" method on the Printco_printer class and the "print" method on the Xcorp_printer class? They do exactly the same thing—they both send a print job to the printer.

Printco_printer	submit_job
	queue_status
	flush_job
	...
Xcorp_printer	print
	show_jobs
	cancel_job
	flush
	...

Figure 5-5 Too many methods

Now let's say a security administrator is responsible for two printers—a Printco printer called "laser1" and an Xcorp printer called "Xjet." If the administrator wants to let a subject called "Joe" print on both printers, he's going to have to write two rules:

> **Joe** may do **submit_job** to **laser1**.

> **Joe** may do **print** to **Xjet**.

This is bad enough when the administrator is setting up the policy for the first time. It's much worse when he wants to go back and change the policy: he has to remember that there are *two* rules which allow Joe to print!

Third, different methods may have similar names

The third problem is that methods on different objects might have *similar* names but *different* functions. Look back at Figure 5-5. The Printco printer has a method called "flush_job"; this cancels the printing of a single document. It will only work if the user who calls it is the one who submitted the job in the first place. The Xcorp printer supports this function too: Its name for the method that does this is "cancel_job."

But look closely; you'll see that the Xcorp printer has another method called "flush." What does this method do? It cancels all the jobs in the printer's queue, regardless of who submitted them. Normally this is the kind of function only a printer administrator should have access to (otherwise users will start canceling each other's jobs!). But our security administrator might very well get confused and give flush permission to all users, thinking that the flush method just flushes a single job (after all, that's what the "flush_job" method does to a Printco printer, and he's administering Printco *and* Xcorp printers).

Administrators need to group methods by sensitivity

All three of these problems exist because method names aren't designed to be useful to security administrators. A method's name describes *what the method does*; but security administrators don't need to know what the method does, they need to know *how dangerous the method is.* So what security administrators really need is a way to group similarly dangerous (or sensitive) methods together and to assign rules to these "sensitivity groups." Figure 5-6 shows an example of this.

CORBAsecurity's **required rights** model provides a way to group methods by sensitivity. It works like this:

Required rights reduce the number of methods for which rules need to be defined

There are four "required rights": **g** ("get"), **s** ("set"), **u** ("use"), and **m** ("manage"). Each of these has an intended meaning. **g** is supposed to be used to control access to methods which return information to the caller; **s** is supposed to be used to control access to methods which change information inside an object; **u** is supposed to be used to control access to methods which cause an object to do some kind of work—maybe a calculation or signaling a device to do something—and **m** is supposed to be used to control access to methods which normal users shouldn't be calling—maybe methods intended for use by system administrators.

Whenever a new interface is defined, its methods are added to a table kept in a special object called *requiredRights*, and each method is assigned a set of required rights. Look at the example in

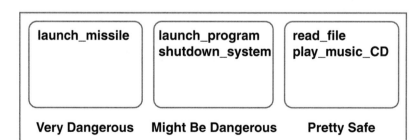

Figure 5-6 Grouping methods by sensitivity

Figure 5-7. The Printco_printer interface has three methods. The first, submit_job, sends a file to the printer to be printed. This changes information inside the Printco_printer object, so it's been assigned the required right "s." The second, queue_status, doesn't change any information inside the Printco_printer object, but it does return information about what's in the printer's queue to the caller, so it's been assigned the required right "g." The third, flush_job, removes a job from the printer's queue. Not only does this change information inside the Printco_printer object, but using it might make people mad. Therefore it's been assigned the "m" required right as well as the "s" required right.

Figure 5-7 Required rights

requiredRights		
Printco_printer	submit_job	s
	queue_status	g
	flush_job	sm
	...	
Xcorp_printer	print	s
	show_jobs	g
	cancel_job	sm
	flush	sm
	...	

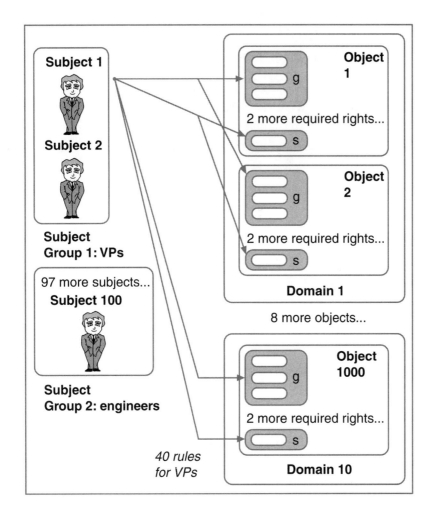

Figure 5-8 Just the
right amount of
access control
policy

Inside the figure:

Subject 1

Subject 2

Subject
Group 1: VPs

97 more subjects...
Subject 100

Subject
Group 2: engineers

40 rules
for VPs

Object 1

g

2 more required rights...

s

Object 2

g

2 more required rights...

s

Domain 1

8 more objects...

Object 1000

g

2 more required rights...

s

Domain 10

Once required rights have been assigned to each of an interface's
methods, security administrators can forget about the methods and
write policy rules using just the four required rights. Look at
Figure 5-8. The security administrator could set up a policy for
domain 1 which says

*Required rights
allow the same policy
to be applied to
objects of
different types*

VPs may do **invoke** to **any method with required-right g**.

VPs may not do **invoke** to **any method with required-right s**.

Using required rights in policy rules has a big advantage over using method names. Even though **object1** and **object2** might not have the same set of method names, they will always have the same set of required rights. This means that the same policy rule can be used for both of them, since policy rules don't need to mention method names. So in a system which uses required rights, security administrators can control a subject's access to all the objects in a domain using just one rule—even if the objects all have different sets of methods.

Look at Figure 5-8 again; you'll see that using privilege attributes, domains, and required rights has reduced a system with 100 subjects, 1000 objects, and as many as 10,000 actions to one with 2 subjects, 10 objects, and 4 actions, for a total of 80 rules—much better than 1,000,000!

Enforcing Access Control Policy

Now that we've seen what access control policy looks like, we'll take a look at how the system enforces it.

In Chapter 3, we saw how ORBs enforce policy by intercepting messages and calling policy enforcement code. The policy enforcement code that makes access-control decisions in CORBAsecurity systems lives inside **accessDecision** objects, as Figure 5-9 shows.

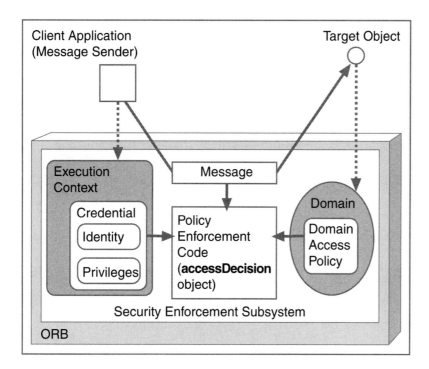

Figure 5-9 ORBs use
accessDecision
objects to make
access decisions

The accessDecision Procedure

The ORB and an accessDecision object (ADO) go through a 6-step process to make and enforce an access decision:

Step 1: ORB asks ADO for an access decision

When the ORB gets a message, it asks an accessDecision object to decide whether the subject sending the message should be allowed to invoke the requested method on the message's target object. The accessDecision object performs steps 2 through 5 to make a decision.

ORBs use accessDecision objects to make access decisions

Step 2: ADO gets policy from domain

AccessDecision objects get policies from domains

As Figure 5-9 shows, accessDecision objects get access control policies from target objects' domains. Each domain has exactly one access control policy object.

Step 3: ADO gets subject's granted rights from policy

Access control policy objects tell the system which rights each subject has to all the objects in a domain. Access control policy rules have the following general form:

> **subject** is granted **rights <rights list>**

Subjects in an access control policy rule are privilege attributes; rights are drawn from the standard set of required rights. So the rules in a real access control policy object might look like this:

> **printer-admin** is granted **rights g**, **s**, and **m**
>
> **VPs** are granted **rights g** and **s**
>
> **engineers** are granted **rights s**

AccessDecision objects get granted rights from policies

The accessDecision object passes the subject's security attributes to the domain's policy object; the policy object returns the subject's granted rights.

Step 4: ADO gets required rights for method

Remember from earlier in this chapter that the requiredRights object keeps a table defining which rights are required to invoke each of an object's methods. Since the accessDecision object knows which object is the target of the subject's message, it can figure out which interface and method is being invoked and ask the required-Rights object for the list of rights required to invoke that interface and method.

Using the example in Figure 5-10, the accessDecision object might call the requiredRights object and ask for the rights required to invoke the flush_job method of the Printco_printer interface. The requiredRights object would return a list of rights with a **combinator**. The combinator tells the accessDecision object whether *all* the rights in the list must be granted, or whether *any* one of the rights in the list is sufficient. Here's the list the requiredRights object returns to the accessDecision object (still using the example in Figure 5-10) when it asks for the flush_job method's required rights:

AccessDecision objects get the list of rights needed to invoke a specific method

all: s, m

Step 5: ADO compares granted rights with required rights

To make a decision, the accessDecision object simply compares the granted rights it gets back from an access control **policy** object to the required rights it gets back from the requiredRights object.

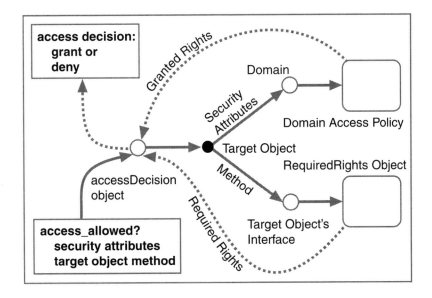

access decision: grant or deny

Granted Rights

Domain

Security Attributes

Domain Access Policy

RequiredRights Object

accessDecision object

Target Object

Method

Target Object's Interface

Required Rights

access_allowed?
security attributes
target object method

Figure 5-10 Access control decision procedure

AccessDecision objects compare granted rights to required rights to make a decision

If the required rights have been granted to the subject, then the accessDecision object's decision will be **grant**; otherwise it will be **deny**. The accessDecision object returns its decision to the ORB.

Step 6: ORB enforces policy

The ORB receives the decision. If the decision is "grant," the ORB invokes the requested method on the target object and returns the result to the subject. If the decision is "deny," the ORB refuses to invoke the method.

Figure 5-10 summarizes how access control decisions are made.

Combining Policies to Make Access Decisions

Even though each domain has only one access control policy object, an object can still have more than one access control policy because objects can belong to more than one domain.

Objects can belong to several domains

Figure 5-11 shows a couple of ways this can happen. The black dots in the picture are objects; the white circles are domains.

The left-hand side of the picture shows two objects which are members of **hierarchical domains**. Each of these objects is a direct member of only one domain, but that domain itself belongs to another domain. Hierarchical domains can be **centralized**, which means that if the policy of a domain higher in the tree conflicts with the policy of a domain lower in the tree, the higher policy wins, or they can be **autonomous**, which means that the lower policy wins.

The right-hand side of the figure shows an object which is a direct member of two different domains. Since the object belongs to both

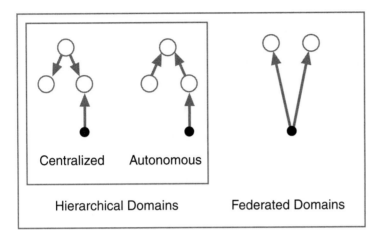

Figure 5-11 Domain relationships

domains, both domains' policies apply to it. Because both policies apply, there needs to be a rule to take care of cases where the policies don't agree. This rule is called a **federation agreement**, and domains with federation agreements are called **federated domains**.

When an object is a member of more than one domain, it's up to the accessDecision object to decide how to reconcile the different domains' policies. The CORBAsecurity model doesn't define any rules for doing this, so different accessDecision objects might do it in different ways.

AccessDecision objects combine the results from all applicable policies to make a decision

Figure 5-12 shows an example of one way an accessDecision object might combine several domains' policies to arrive at a decision. The small black dot in the figure represents an object which belongs to four domains (an arrow connects the object to each of the domains it belongs to). Domain 1 is part of a centralized hierarchy, which means that its policy can be overridden by its superior domain (domain 5). Domain 2 is part of a hierarchy with local autonomy,

**Figure 5-12
Reconciling
decisions from
different domains'
policies**

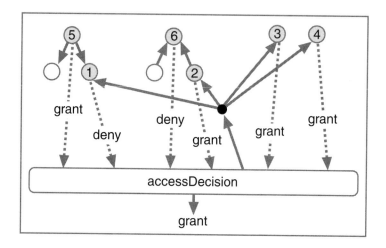

which means that its superior domain's policy 6 will apply only if it does not have a rule that applies to this decision. Domains 3 and 4 are autonomous, which means that only their own policies will apply.

Domain 1's policy would deny access, but it's overridden by domain 5's grant. Domain 2's grant makes domain 6's result irrelevant. Domain 3 grants, and domain 4 denies. How does the accessDecision object combine these four results (three grants and a deny)? CORBAsecurity doesn't specify this; different accessDecision objects are free to combine results in different ways, in order to support a range of different policy options. In Figure 5-12, the rule the accessDecision object enforces might be "as long as a majority of the domains' policies grant, return grant as the decision."

6

Message Protection

In Chapter 5, we saw that access control protects information inside objects by refusing to let subjects invoke methods they're not allowed to use. Since methods are the only way to get information out of an object (or change information inside an object), access control protection works as long as information stays inside an object.

But once information passes out of an object and into a message (by being returned in response to a "get" method invocation, for example), subjects can do things to it without using methods. Sneaky subjects can look at messages going back and forth on network wires and read the information in them, looking for interesting things they're not supposed to know about. Even sneakier subjects can change messages as they go back and forth on the wire, hoping that the changed information will be written back into objects and will confuse honest subjects who use those objects later.

Object security systems need to protect messages so that unauthorized subjects can't read or change information in them. This is what **message protection** is for.

Message protection protects information outside of objects

Message protection, like access control, is enforced based on policy. Message protection policy specifies what **quality of protection** (or **QOP**) needs to be applied to each message. In Chapter 3 we saw how ORBs enforce policy by intercepting messages and calling policy enforcement code. The policy enforcement code which enforces message protection policy lives inside **securityContext** objects. Figure 6-1 shows how the ORB uses securityContext objects to enforce message protection policy.

Managing Message Protection Policy

Message protection policy defines what should be done to a message to protect it against unauthorized access when it's transmitted. Message protection policy is stored in QOP objects.

Quality of Protection

ORBs can enforce three different kinds of message protection:

- **Message origin authentication** proves the identity of the sender of the message to the receiver.

Figure 6-1 Message protection

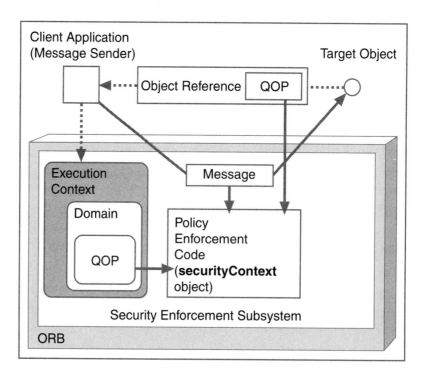

- **Message confidentiality** prevents unauthorized subjects from reading the message's data.
- **Message integrity** prevents unauthorized subjects from changing the message's data.

A QOP object defines which of these kinds of protection should be applied to a message. A message could be protected using all three kinds of protection, or just one or two kinds, or none at all.

Quality of protection defines what kind of protection a message needs

Message protection is usually implemented using encryption. In some systems it may not be necessary for the ORB to encrypt information to protect it, however.

Message protection is usually implemented using encryption . . .

ORBs which run over Virtual Private Network links, for example, may assume that message confidentiality and message integrity are guaranteed by the virtual private network's encryption services. In this case, the ORB doesn't need to do any additional encryption, even if the message protection policy says that message confidentiality and message integrity are required.

. . . but not always!

Defining Message Protection Policy

Message protection policy can be defined by object owners, by system owners, and by subjects. Object owners use message protection to guarantee that data flowing into and out of their objects is adequately protected. System owners use message protection to guarantee that messages flowing through ORBs on their systems are adequately protected. And subjects use message protection policies to guarantee that the messages they send and receive are adequately protected.

Many people can define message protection policies

This might seem like a lot of policy, but there are good reasons to allow all three groups of people to have their own policies. Let's look at an example. Imagine a server called `info.cia.mil`. The administrator of this server might decide that all messages sent to this server must be authenticated so that he can find out who sent them. On the other hand, he might want to be able to get messages from anyone—even people who can't or won't encrypt their messages. Now imagine a document storage application running on `info.cia.mil`. This application receives reports from subjects and stores them as objects. The document storage administrator might decide that all messages sent to the document storage application must be integrity protected, to guarantee that no reports can be tampered with by wiretappers. Finally, imagine a subject called "James Bond." James might decide that all messages he sends to his American colleagues at the CIA should be encrypted so that Ernst Stavro Blofeld can't read them as they sing across the wires.

An object's owner can require messages sent to it to be protected

Object owners can define message protection policies for their objects. The ORB won't accept a message which has been sent to an object unless the message has been protected as strongly as the object owner's message protection policy requires.

Object owners' message protection policies are stored in object references

When an object's owner defines a message protection policy, a description of the policy is written into the object's reference so that callers will know what protection they need to apply in order to send messages to the object (see Figure 6-1). An object owner's message protection policy defines the minimum protection the owner will permit and the maximum protection the owner's system can support.

A system's owner can require messages it sends or receives to be protected

System owners can define two kinds of message protection policies:

Client secure invocation policy defines the minimum protection which must be applied to messages sent from the system.

Server secure invocation policy defines both the minimum protection which must be applied to messages received by the system and the maximum protection the system can support.

When a system owner defines either of these types of message protection policies, a policy object is created and attached to the Current object representing the active execution context.

System message protection policies are stored in secure invocation policy objects

Subjects can define message protection policies to control what level of protection is applied to messages they send and receive. They may require a minimum level of protection to be applied to all messages they send and receive, and they may specify a maximum level of protection they are prepared to accept.

A subject can require messages he sends or receives to be protected

When a subject defines a message protection policy, a description of the policy is written into the subject's Credential object.

Subject message protection policies are stored in Credential objects

Enforcing Message Protection Policy

Having three different sets of message protection policies gives the ORB a complicated job; it's got to look at system, object owner, and subject policies and find a QOP setting that satisfies all three policies.

Here's how the ORB combines message protection policies to come up with the QOP it actually applies to a message.

The ORB combines message protection policies to determine the required effective quality of protection

1. If the ORB is going to send a message, it needs to consider the subject's policy (found in the subject's credential), the object owner's policy (from the object reference), and the system owner's policy (which can be found in the client secure invocation policy object on the Current object that represents the currently active execution context).

   • The subject policy, object owner policy, and system owner policy will each specify a required QOP. The ORB combines these three policies to determine the *required effective QOP*; any kind of protection required by one or more of the three policies will be required by the required effective QOP also.

For example, if any of the three policies requires integrity, the required effective QOP will require message integrity.

- The object owner policy will specify a maximum supported QOP. The ORB checks to make sure that the required effective QOP built in the previous step can be supported by the object owner's system. If the required effective QOP calls for a kind of protection the object owner policy does *not* support, then the ORB will refuse to send the message because either the subject or the system owner has specified a quality of protection the receiving system can't handle.

- If the object owner's system can support the required effective QOP, the ORB creates a securityContext object which will implement the required effective QOP.

The ORB creates a
securityContext object

This securityContext object will handle the actual protection of the message (we'll describe this in more detail later). Figure 6-2 shows how the ORB combines message protection policies before sending a message.

2. If the ORB has received a message, it needs to consider the QOP the sender applied to the message (found in a *context setup token* sent along with the message), the receiving subject's policy (from the receiving subject's credential), and the system owner's policy (which can be found in the server secure invocation policy object on the Current object representing the currently active execution context).

- The receiving subject's policy and system owner policy will each specify a required QOP. The ORB combines these two policies with the sender's applied policy to determine the *accepted effective QOP*; any kind of protection specified by one or more of the three policies will be required by the accepted effective QOP also. For example, if either of the two policies or the sender's applied QOP requires integrity, the accepted effective QOP will require message integrity.

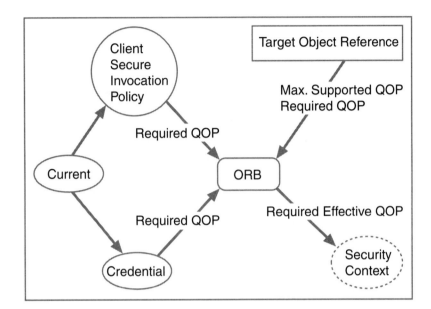

- The receiving subject's policy and the system owner policy will each specify a maximum supported QOP. The ORB checks to make sure that the accepted effective QOP built in the previous step can be supported by both the object owner's system and the receiving subject. If the accepted effective QOP calls for a kind of protection which either of these does *not* support, then the ORB will refuse to receive the message. If the receiving system and the receiving subject both can support the required effective QOP, the ORB creates a securityContext object which will implement the accepted effective QOP.

Figure 6-3 shows how an ORB combines message protection policies when it receives a message.

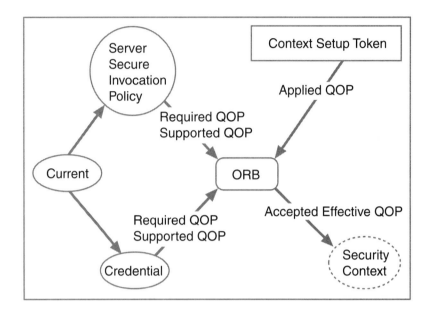

Once the ORB has created a securityContext object which implements the required QOP, it simply passes messages that need to be
protected to the securityContext object.

*SecurityContext
objects protect
messages*

The securityContext object applies whatever protection is required
(this usually involves encrypting all or part of the message) and
passes the protected message back to the ORB. The ORB then sends
the protected message. Figure 6-4 shows how the ORB uses
securityContext objects to protect messages.

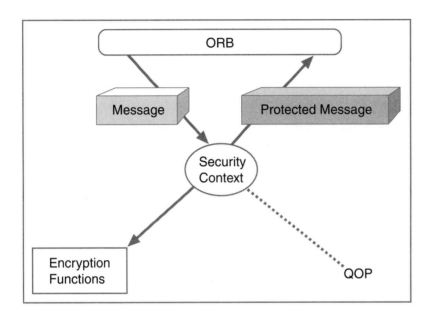

Figure 6-4 Security-
Context objects
protect messages

7

Delegation

In an object system, a request may pass through many objects on many different computers before it arrives at its final destination. Regardless of how many objects and servers the request passes through, the destination object's ORB may want to know the identity of the original sender of the message before it decides to accept the request and act on it.

Delegation allows an object to "pass along" a caller's identity to another object so that the original sender's identity remains with a request throughout its journey to its final destination.

Delegation allows users to pass their identities to objects they call

The Secure Proxy Problem

Object systems often build complicated functions by gluing together objects with simpler functions. Here's a simple example: Imagine that a bank has built a very simple account management class called "AcctObj." Each instance of this class represents a user's savings and checking accounts. It allows the user who owns the account to deposit to and withdraw from each of his accounts (the bank's access control policy prevents use of an instance of AcctObj by anyone except the account's owner). Figure 7-1 shows a user named Bill managing his accounts using AcctObj.

Now let's consider one of the bank's customers—call him Bill. Bill can use his AcctObj to move money into and out of his accounts. Bill may be satisfied with the service AcctObj provides for a while,

Figure 7-1 A simple
user account
application

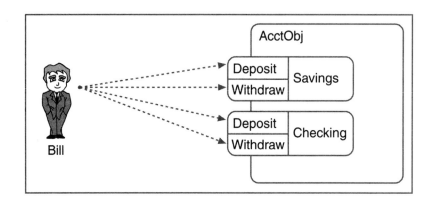

but pretty soon he'll want to do something more complicated, like
transferring money from his savings account to his checking
account. AcctObj doesn't provide a transfer function, so Bill will
have to withdraw from savings and then deposit to checking to
complete the transfer. This is a little inconvenient; after a while Bill
might become unhappy with the bank's services. Bill could decide
to move his accounts to a bank that provides a transfer function.
But what if Bill's a programmer? He might decide to write his own
funds transfer application instead of switching banks. Figure 7-2
shows what Bill's transfer function (XferApp) might look like.

Figure 7-2 The funds
transfer application

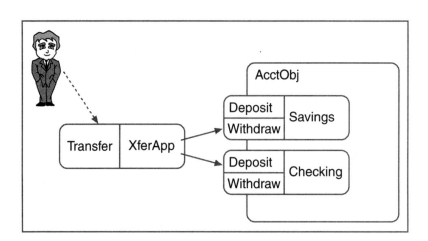

When Bill runs his new XferApp program from his home computer, the program runs under his credentials.

Remember our discussion of execution contexts in Chapter 4? When Bill authenticates himself, his identity and privilege attributes are stored in his *own credential*. That credential is also used as the *invocation credential*, which is sent to the bank's server along with Bill's request. When the bank's server gets Bill's request, it takes the credential and puts it into the *received credential* slot in its own execution context. Then it uses the received credential information to do an access control check (remember Chapter 5) to make sure that it's really Bill who's trying to withdraw money from Bill's savings account. (See Figure 7-3.)

When a user runs a program, the program gets the user's identity

So far, so good. Since it really is Bill calling, he'll pass the bank's access control check, and the transfer will work.

Now let's say Bill gets a call from the bank's Information Services director. The IS director has heard that Bill has built a transfer

A program which gets the user's credential will get the user's permissions

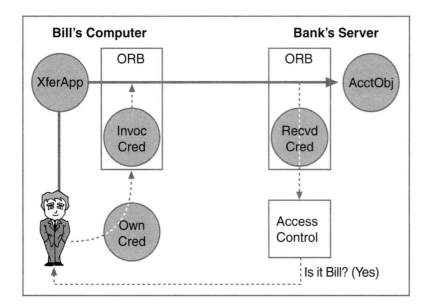

Figure 7-3 The funds transfer application inheriting the user's identity

application. He's getting a lot of calls from other customers who are threatening to switch banks unless he provides a transfer function (the other customers aren't programmers, so they can't build their own). The IS director would like to buy Bill's application and install it at the bank. After a bit of negotiation, Bill agrees to the deal and hands over the code for XferApp.

The bank's IS director installs XferApp on one of his servers, as Figure 7-4 shows.

Bill cashes his check and goes home happy—for an hour. Then the IS director calls him back and tells him that XferApp doesn't work.

Objects a user calls remotely don't get the user's identity . . .

Bill goes to his computer, runs XferApp, and confirms that it works. But the IS director is adamant—it isn't working for any of the bank's other customers. Bill suspects that the bank may have changed something and broken his program, so he tries using the bank's version of XferApp—the one on the Transfer Server. Sure enough, it doesn't work! It gives Bill an "Access Denied" message.

Figure 7-4 The funds transfer application running on the bank's server

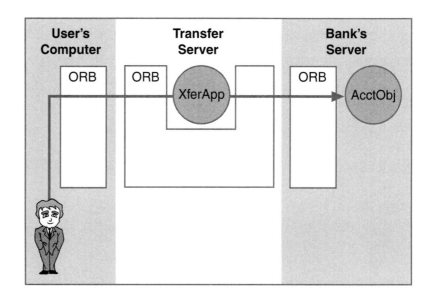

Bill calls the IS director. He says the bank must have changed something and broken XferApp. But the IS director denies it. The bank followed Bill's instructions for installing and running XferApp to the letter and didn't change anything.

Bill goes down to the bank. After a lot of debugging, he figures out that XferApp is failing the bank's access control check when it's running on the Transfer Server because the Transfer Server is using its own credentials instead of the user's credentials.

. . . they get the identity of the server they're running on . . .

Figure 7-5 shows the details of what happens when Bill uses the version of XferApp running on the bank's Transfer Server.

Bill logs on to his computer. This establishes his *own credential*. By default, this credential becomes his *invocation credential*, which is passed to the Transfer Server along with Bill's request. Bill's request activates XferApp.

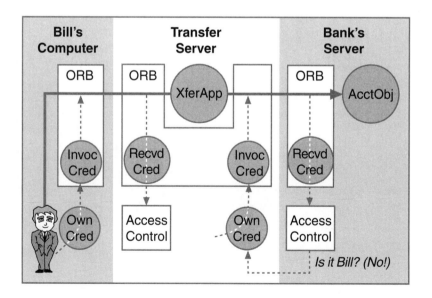

Figure 7-5 The funds transfer application using its own identity

But XferApp has its own execution context containing the Transfer Server's credentials. The Transfer Server's *own credential* was established some time before XferApp was activated and will be used by default as the Transfer Server's *invocation credential*. So when XferApp calls Bill's AcctObj on the bank's server, the credential passed along with the request will be the Transfer Server's credential.

. . . so objects a user calls remotely don't get the user's permissions

This credential will be used as the bank's server's *received credential.* When the bank's server uses its received credential to do an access control check, access will be denied because only Bill (and not the Transfer Server) is permitted to use Bill's AcctObj.

Users sometimes need to pass their identities to objects they call remotely

The IS director wants Bill to fix XferApp. To do this, Bill needs a way to get XferApp to pass the user's credential to the bank's server. To do this, the Transfer Server is going to have to turn its *received credential* (which is really the user's credential, of course) into its *invocation credential* (see Figure 7-6).

Figure 7-6 The funds transfer application passing on the user's identity

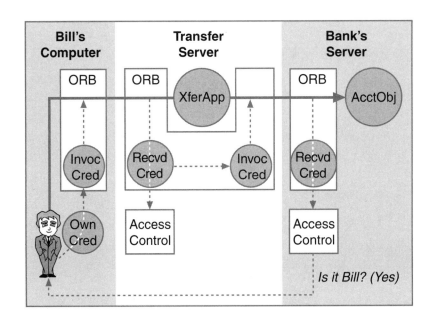

The act of turning a received credential into an invocation credential is called **delegation**.

The owner of the original credential is called the **initiator** of the request.

Each receiver of a delegated request is called an **intermediate**; if an intermediate chooses to turn the initiator's received credential into its invocation credential, it becomes a **delegate**.

The final recipient of the request (the object that performs the requested operation) is called the **target** of the request.

In our example, Bill is the initiator, the Transfer Server containing the XferApp is an intermediate and a delegate, and Bill's AcctObj on the bank's server is the target.

A delegate can pass a request on to another delegate, so the request can travel through a whole **chain** of delegates, one after another, before it reaches its final destination. Each delegate in the chain passes the initiator's credential on to the next delegate in the chain, until the last delegate passes it on to the target.

Managing Delegation Policy

Initiators, intermediates, and targets may all have delegation policies.

Initiator Policy. Each initiator has to decide whether or not to allow its credentials to be delegated.

Delegation enables users to pass their identities to objects they call

A delegation chain starts with an initiator (usually a user) . . .

. . . passes through some number of delegates . . .

. . . and ends at a target

There's no limit to the number of delegates in a delegation chain

Every member of a delegation chain can have a delegation policy

*Initiators use policy
to control who gets to
use their identities*

This is important because once you've given your identity away, it's hard to get it back. Untrustworthy delegates might use an initiator's credentials to do things the initiator doesn't approve of (in our example, a rogue version of the XferApp could withdraw all the money from Bill's savings and checking accounts and send it to a third party). So it's important for initiators to make sure that their credentials can be used only by delegates they trust.

An initiator can control whether its credentials can be delegated by setting the **DelegationMode** on its invocation credential.

- If DelegationMode = **Delegate**, then the receiver of the credentials may delegate them.
- If DelegationMode = **NoDelegate**, then the receiver may not delegate the credentials.

*Intermediates use
delegation policy to
control when they
use their callers'
identities . . .*

Intermediate Policy. Each intermediate has to decide when it should pass on the initiator's credentials and when it should use its own credentials.

In general, if the intermediate is accessing a target its caller asked for, it will want to become a delegate and use the initiator's received credential.

*. . . and when they
use their own
identities*

If it's accessing a target it needs for its own purposes, it should use its own credential.

Intermediates have two ways to control delegation:

*Intermediates can set
up a default
delegation policy . . .*

An initiator can set up the default delegation mode for all its invocations by setting the **Delegation Policy** for its execution context's domain (if you've forgotten about execution contexts and their domains, look back at Chapters 2 and 4). The Delegation policy can be set to one of three values:

- **NoDelegation:** The intermediate will use its own credentials.

- **SimpleDelegation:** The intermediate will pass on the initiator's received credentials.
- **CompositeDelegation:** The intermediate will pass both its own credentials and the initiator's received credentials.

A different delegation mode can be chosen for each class. An intermediate could choose, for example, to use the initiator's credential for access to objects of the AcctObj class, but to use its own credential for access to objects of other classes.

An intermediate can override the default delegation policy by setting the **delegation mode security feature** of its invocation credential. This feature has the same three values as the delegation policy.

. . . and they can override the default policy for specific messages

Target Policy. Targets' ORBs may choose to consider the delegation mode when they make access control decisions.

Access control policies may grant or deny access based on delegation mode. For example, an access control policy could grant access if Bill is the requester and the request was not delegated, but deny access if Bill is the requester and the request was delegated.

Targets use delegation policy to decide whether to accept delegated requests

Access control policies can also base policy decisions on the identities of the delegates (if CompositeDelegation was used). For example, an access control policy could grant access only if the initiator and all the delegates in the chain are allowed to access the target.

Enforcing Delegation Policy

The ORB enforces all delegation policies

The ORB enforces all delegation policies:

Enforcing initiator policy. The initiator's ORB marks the invocation credential with the user's selected DelegationMode. If the selected mode is NoDelegate, then intermediates will not be able to pass the credential on. If the selected mode is Delegate, then intermediates will be able to become delegates and pass the credential on.

The user's ORB enforces initiator delegation policy

Enforcing intermediate policy. If an intermediate selects SimpleDelegation or CompositeDelegation mode, its ORB will try to use the initiator's received credential as its invocation credential. This will succeed if the initiator's received credential was marked as delegatable; otherwise, it will fail.

Intermediate objects' ORBs enforce intermediate delegation policies

Enforcing target policy. Target policy is enforced at the time an access control decision is made (look back at Chapter 5 if you don't remember the details of how an access control decision is made). The target's ORB will pass the received credential, with its delegation mode marker, to an accessDecision object. The accessDecision object, in turn, will pass the credential to the domainAccessPolicy object for each domain the target object belongs to. Each domainAccessPolicy object will take the delegation mode into account when it returns the requester's granted rights.

The target's ORB and accessPolicy enforce target delegation policy

8

Security Auditing

Security auditing is the process of checking a system to see whether it's been set up securely, whether it's being used securely, and whether it's being attacked.

An **audit service** makes security auditing easier by generating a little report (called an **audit event**) every time something happens that a security auditor might want to know about. Audit events can be displayed on a screen, stored in a log file, or sent as messages, depending on how often the auditor wants to receive reports and how she wants to read them.

Security auditing tells you what's going on in your system

If the audit service generated an audit event every time anything happened in the system, huge numbers of events would be generated. The system would slow down because it would be spending a lot of its time creating audit events. If audit events were stored on disk, the disk would fill up quickly. If audit events were transmitted elsewhere, the system's communications channels might become clogged with audit event data.

Too much auditing is a bad thing

Fortunately, most of the things that happen in a computer system aren't significant from a security auditor's point of view. The audit service doesn't need to generate an audit event unless something important happens (like when somebody tries the wrong password several times, or when somebody deletes an important file).

The audit service looks at everything that happens in the system; each time something happens, the audit service looks at the

Audit policy lets you audit only the important events

security administrator's **audit policy** to figure out what (if anything) it should do.

Managing Audit Policy

Every time something happens in the system, the audit service needs to decide whether or not to generate an audit event. To make this decision, it consults an **audit event generation policy**.

Event Generation Policy

Audit event generation policies give a security auditor a lot of control over when the audit service generates audit events.

AuditPolicy objects control which system events are audited

CORBAsecurity systems store audit policies in **AuditPolicy objects**. Each AuditPolicy object has a set of **audit selectors**, which it uses to decide whether a particular system event should result in the creation of an audit event.

Audit selectors define policy for specific types of system events

Each audit selector tells the audit service what to do when a particular type of system event happens. Each time a system event happens, the audit service looks through the audit policy to see if it has a selector for the type of event that occurred. If there's no selector for that type of system event, no audit event will be generated. CORBAsecurity lets administrators create selectors for these system event types:

- Principal authentication (user logons)
- Session authentication (creating secure connections)
- Authorization (access control checks)
- Invocation (sending a message)
- Change in security environment
- Change in security policy
- Object creation
- Object destruction
- Non-repudiation
- All events

If the audit policy has an audit selector for the the type of system event that happened, the selector will contain a **value list**. The value list will specify one or more of the following values:

- The target's interface type
- The target's object reference
- The requested operation
- The initiator's credential
- Whether the operation succeeded or failed
- The time

The audit service should generate an audit event if the system event matches all the values in the selector's value list.

In a CORBA object system, security administrators can define three kinds of audit event generation policies:

Client invocation audit policies govern which object invocations cause audit events to be generated by the client's ORB.

Target invocation audit policies govern which object invocations cause audit events to be generated by the target's ORB.

Application audit policies govern which object invocations cause applications to generate audit events.

Enforcing Audit Policy

Each time a message is sent, the sender's ORB calls an **AuditDecision object** to see whether it needs to generate an audit event. The AuditDecision object makes its decision by comparing the request values to the relevant audit selectors in the client invocation audit policy object for the current execution context.

AuditDecision objects make AuditPolicy decisions

Each time a message is received, the target object's ORB calls an AuditDecision object to see whether it needs to generate an audit event. The AuditDecision object makes its decision by comparing the request values to the relevant audit selectors in the target invocation audit policy object for the target object.

When an application object receives a message, it may choose to call an AuditDecision object to see whether it needs to generate an audit event. The AuditDecision object makes its decision by comparing the request values to the relevant audit selectors in an application audit policy object for the target object.

ORBs and applications enforce audit policy decisions

If an ORB or application asks an AuditDecision object whether it needs to generate an audit event and it gets a "yes" answer, the ORB or application is responsible for enforcing the decision. It does this by calling an AuditChannel object and asking it to generate the required audit event.

Audit Decisions

AuditDecision objects use AuditPolicy objects to decide whether an audit event should be generated for a particular system event.

AuditDecision objects compare system event data to audit policy

When an ORB or application calls an AuditDecision object to ask whether an audit event needs to be generated, it passes a list of selector values, which describe the system event that happened, to the AuditDecision object. The AuditDecision object compares these selector values against the relevant selector value list in the appropriate AuditPolicy object and returns a "yes" or "no." If it returns a "yes," then the ORB or application needs to generate an audit event, as Figure 8-1 shows.

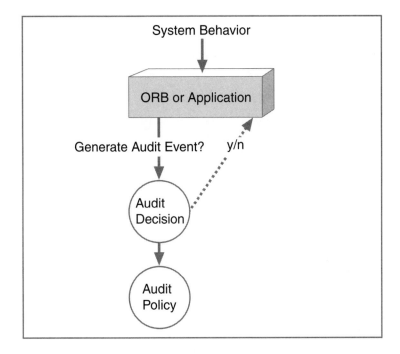

Figure 8-1
The AuditDecision
object decides
whether to generate
an audit event

Audit Channels

If the ORB or application needs to generate an audit event, it first
needs to locate an AuditChannel object. To do this, it goes to the
AuditDecision object which told it to generate an audit event and
asks it which AuditChannel object to use, as Figure 8-2 shows.
Once it's got the right AuditChannel object, it creates an audit event
by passing some data describing the system event to the Audit-
Channel object. The data which the ORB or application passes to
the AuditChannel object includes:

- The event type
- The event initiator's credentials
- The time the event occurred
- The selector values passed to the AuditDecision object
- (Optionally) other event-specific data

Figure 8-2
The AuditDecision
object specifies an
AuditChannel

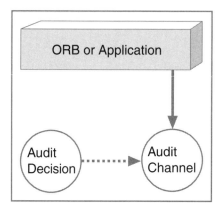

The AuditChannel object packages this data into a standard audit event format and disposes of it.

Audit information can be used in many ways

There are many ways to dispose of audit events. They could, for example, be written into a log file on disk. They could be sent as alarms to a system operator's screen. They could be sent to a security manager's pager. The event could even be ignored and thrown away.

Audit channels decide what to do with the events they receive

CORBAsecurity doesn't specify what action an audit channel should take when it disposes of an audit event. Implementors of CORBAsecurity audit services are free to do anything they want. Different AuditChannel objects are even free to do different things with the same event. Figure 8-3 shows an AuditChannel object with three ways to dispose of events.

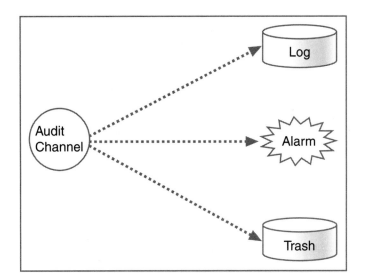

Figure 8-3 The
AuditChannel
disposes of
audit events

9

Non-Repudiation

Non-repudiation services generate evidence which will help to convince a disinterested third party that a specific subject performed a specific action. This chapter describes how a non-repudiation service works and what policies it can support.

Disputes, Evidence, and the Burden of Proof

Disputes

A **dispute** arises when one party makes an accusation against a second party, and the second party denies the accusation. When a dispute arises, it needs to be settled. Many disputes are settled by appeal to a disinterested third party who will examine evidence supporting the accusation and evidence casting doubt on the accusation.

Disputes are settled by presenting evidence to arbitrators

There are different kinds of accusations, and evidence will be used differently depending on what kind of accusation has been made.

Evidence is used differently in different circumstances

If the accuser claims that the accused did something bad, then the "burden of proof" will usually fall on the accuser—he'll be the one who has to produce the evidence.

A party who accuses another of doing something bad may be required to produce non-repudiation evidence that shows that the accused committed the offense. If the accuser has evidence, he can use it to argue that the accused is guilty. But if there isn't any evidence, the accusation may not be believed.

If the accuser claims that the accused failed to do something which was required, then the "burden of proof" will usually fall on the accused—he'll be the one who has to produce the evidence.

A party who is accused of failing to do something which was required may be given the chance to show non-repudiation evidence that he did what he was supposed to do. If the accused party has evidence, he can use it to argue that the accusation is false. But if he can't produce any evidence, the accusation may be believed.

Non-Repudiation Evidence

Non-repudiation services generate evidence of subjects' actions

Non-repudiation services work by generating **evidence** of subjects' actions. When a dispute arises, non-repudiation evidence can be used to help settle the issue.

Non-repudiation protection will be effective if transactions are designed to assure the following:

Non-repudiation evidence should tell the truth about likely disputes

- Each party has evidence to cast doubt on all *false* accusations that might be made against it.
- Each party has evidence to support all *true* accusations it might want to make.
- No party has evidence to support any false accusation it might want to make.

When a disagreement happens and there's non-repudiation evidence available, the evidence has to be evaluated by whoever is responsible for making a decision. Normally this will be an impartial third party—a mediator or a judge, for example.

Arbitrators use evidence to settle disputes

Trusted third parties who evaluate non-repudiation evidence are called **arbitrators**. Arbitrators have to have rules for evaluating evidence so that all the parties to the disagreement will believe they're being treated fairly. Rules of evidence can come from lots of different sources. The rules judges use, for example, are defined by civil and criminal laws, but the rules mediators use may be less strictly defined.

Using the rules of evidence as a guide, an arbitrator will allow (or require) the parties to a disagreement to submit various kinds of evidence. After evidence has been submitted, the arbitrator will check it to decide whether or not it's trustworthy.

Lots of things could be submitted to an arbitrator as evidence. But not everything that could be submitted would be useful. Some things might even be rejected because the rules of evidence don't allow them to be used. When an arbitrator needs to settle a disagreement about a business transaction, a few kinds of evidence are especially useful:

- **Evidence of Origination** establishes that a subject originated the text of a particular message (for example, a contract, an offer, or a payment authorization).
- **Evidence of Submission** establishes that a subject submitted a particular message to be sent.
- **Evidence of Receipt** establishes that a subject received a particular message.

Each of these kinds of evidence needs to identify which subject or subjects were involved in the action (for example, "Joe submitted a letter to the U.S. Postal Service"). It's usually helpful to have the evidence include the time the action happened. The place where the action happened may also need to be included (sometimes arbitrators need to know where the action happened so that they can decide whether or not they have the **jurisdiction** to settle the disagreement).

Three types of non-repudiation evidence are especially useful

Non-Repudiation Policies

Every party in a transaction may have a non-repudiation policy

Each participant in a transaction (the sender and receiver of messages or goods, any trusted third parties—like notaries, delivery services, and so on—supporting the transaction, and any arbitrators who may have to settle disputes about the transaction) may have a non-repudiation policy. Different kinds of parties have different kinds of policies:

- Senders' and receivers' policies specify what kinds of evidence should be generated.

Senders and receivers use evidence to protect themselves

Let's say Sally is considering buying a copy of *Wuthering Heights* over the Internet from BookWarehouse.com. If she decides to buy the book, Sally will be the "sender" in a payment transaction. She may not agree to run the payment program unless she gets a receipt for her payment—in other words, unless she gets non-repudiation evidence of receipt of her payment by the "receiver" (BookWarehouse.com). The receipt will help Sally get her money back if the book doesn't arrive.

Each sender and receiver decides what evidence it requires

BookWarehouse.com, on the other hand, may not agree to send the book to Sally unless it can get a tracking number from the delivery service—in other words, unless it can get non-repudiation evidence of submission of the book to the delivery service. The tracking number will help BookWarehouse.com prove that Sally received the book if she fraudulently asks for her money back after the book has been delivered.

- Trusted third-party policy defines valid evidence.

A digital signature on a document may normally be valid evidence that the signer originated the document, but if the signer's key has been revoked, the signature (and the evidence) may be considered invalid. Trusted third-party policies need to define the rules for revoking keys that protect key owners against theft and misuse of their keys, but at the same time protect receivers of signed documents against false denials by the signers. An example will help to show why rules for revocation are needed.

Let's say that your Platinum Plasticard gets stolen. As soon as you report that your card is missing, Plasticard will cancel the card. But what if the thief used it between the time he stole it and the time you called Plasticard? Let's say he did—he made 100 calls to the International Weather Hotline for $10 each. The International Weather Hotline's credit card records are non-repudiation evidence of origination indicating that *you* made the calls (after all, it was your card!). You'll end up with $1000 of charges you don't want to pay for on your next Plasticard statement.

Non-repudiation evidence isn't proof: It can be challenged

When you get your statement, you call Plasticard and say that you don't want to pay for the International Weather Hotline calls. But Plasticard is suspicious; they think it was really you making the calls, and you're just trying to get out of paying for them by pretending that your card was stolen. They want to take you to court to make you pay the bill. How will the judge decide who's responsible for the charges?

Arbitrators need rules to decide whether evidence is valid

Plasticard is a trusted third party in this case; its card was used to pay for transactions between you (or the thief) and the International Weather Hotline. Plasticard has to have a non-repudiation policy which tells an arbitrator (in this case, a judge) what rules you have to follow if you want to repudiate a transaction that's been paid for using your card. If these rules were followed, then you don't have to pay; otherwise, you do.

Trusted third parties define the rules

Credit card companies today have non-repudiation policies limiting your liability for fraudulent charges. You usually have 24 to 48 hours after you figure out that your card is missing to report that it's gone. If you do this, the credit card company usually won't make you pay for any charges made on the card after you lost it (but before it was canceled); otherwise, you're liable for the charges.

Assuming that this is Plasticard's policy, the judge will want to know when you discovered that your card was missing, and he'll want to know when you called Plasticard to report the theft. If you discovered the theft quickly and called Plasticard within 24 hours, you probably won't have to pay for the $1000 worth of International Weather Hotline calls.

- Arbitrator policy defines complete evidence.

Evidence must be complete to satisfy rules of evidence

Arbitrators' policies define what kinds of evidence need to be presented, and what information needs to be in the evidence presented, to satisfy the rules of evidence that will be used to settle the dispute. Evidence which satisfies the rules of evidence that will be used to evaluate it is called **complete evidence**. An example will help you understand why complete evidence is important.

Some kinds of evidence are not complete

Let's say you go to an arbitrator (a judge) with a signature on a document you claim is your recently deceased uncle's will. The will leaves all of your uncle's property to you. But your uncle's son claims that the document is a forgery: Your uncle really didn't leave a will. He says all the property should go to him, since he's your uncle's only surviving child.

The judge has to decide whether the will is genuine or not. But she can't tell whether the ink marks on the will are really your uncle's signature unless she has a sample signature to compare against the one on the will.

The judge might insist on seeing the signature card on file with your uncle's bank (to verify that the signature on the will really belongs to your uncle) before she accepts the signature as evidence. In other words, the signature on the will is incomplete evidence unless a known legitimate sample of your uncle's signature is also provided.

Additional information is sometimes needed to make evidence complete

Complete evidence is just as important in the electronic world as in the physical world. An arbitrator presented with a digital signature on an electronic purchase order might insist on seeing the signer's digital certificate (to verify that the signature belongs to the signer) and the certifier's revocation list and revocation policy (to insure that the signer's certificate wasn't revoked at the time the digital signature was executed) before she accepts the signature as evidence.

Each arbitrator will have a policy, based on his or her rules of evidence, that defines what will be considered complete evidence.

Arbitrators' policies specify how to make evidence complete

Managing Non-Repudiation Policy

Non-repudiation is complicated, so we'll go through a familiar example to make it a little clearer.

Let's imagine that Joe Taxpayer, who lives in the United States, has just finished his U.S. Individual Income Tax Form 1040 and is getting ready to send it to the U.S. Internal Revenue Service (IRS). Joe is going to use the U.S. Postal Service (USPS) to send his tax return to the IRS. He's going to want evidence that the post office has received his form, so that if the IRS denies receiving it, he can prove that it was sent on time. The IRS, on the other hand, is going to want evidence that it was really Joe who prepared and sent the form, so that if the wrong income was claimed, they can take Joe to court and prove that he defrauded the government out of some of the tax he owed. Finally, let's imagine that everything in this

Filing a tax return by mail involves a lot of non-repudiation evidence

transaction will be electronic: Joe will sign his tax form digitally, the post office will postmark it digitally, and the IRS will process it electronically.

The taxpayer, the IRS, and the post office all have policies

There are a lot of parties in this transaction, and all of them have policies:

Sender Policy

Joe: Submit the return via certified mail, return receipt requested

Joe wants *evidence of submission* to the U.S. Postal Service, with a timestamp indicating when he submitted the tax return. He also wants *evidence of receipt* by the IRS.

Receiver Policies

Post Office: Submitted documents must be countersigned by the USPS time server within 5 minutes of postmark.

The post office wants *evidence of receipt* of Joe's tax return, with a timestamp indicating when it received Joe's return.

IRS: The taxpayer must sign the tax return. The tax return must be postmarked by midnight, 15 April (taxpayer's local time).

The IRS wants *evidence of origination* of the tax return, indicating that Joe was the originator. It also wants *evidence of submission* of the tax return to the post office with a timestamp indicating that the tax return was submitted by the midnight, April 15 deadline.

Trusted Third-Party Policies

Joe's Certification Authority (CA): Joe may repudiate his certificate within 48 hours of discovering that his cryptographic signature key has been lost or stolen.

USPS's CA: The USPS may repudiate its Web server's certificate or its time-server's certificate if it discovers that either key has been compromised, but it must give 30 days' advance notice to repudiate either certificate.

IRS's CA: The IRS may not repudiate its server's certificate.

Arbitrator Policy

U.S. Tax Court: Repudiation status information for all certificates used to verify signatures must be in submitted evidence.

Enforcing Non-Repudiation Policy

Non-Repudiation Credentials

In order to generate non-repudiation evidence, a subject needs to have a **non-repudiation credential**. Non-repudiation credentials contain special information which can be used to show that a particular subject, and no one else, must have generated a non-repudiation evidence token.

Subjects use non-repudiation credentials to generate evidence

Usually the special information in the non-repudiation credential is the subject's private digital signature key.

Non-repudiation credentials usually contain digital signature keys . . .

An evidence token is often a digital signature created using the signature key in the subject's non-repudiation credential.

. . . and non-repudiation evidence is usually a digital signature

Here's a detailed example of how subjects generate non-repudiation evidence

Generating Non-Repudiation Evidence

Joe is hurrying to complete his electronic form 1040 on the evening of April 15 (the U.S. IRS tax filing deadline).

11:04 P.M., 15 April 1999: Signature

Joe signs form 1040 by using his non-repudiation credential to generate an evidence token. The evidence token contains Joe's certificate and his electronic signature.

The IRS's policy requiring the taxpayer's signature on the tax return is now satisfied.

11:57 P.M., 15 April 1999: Submission

Joe submits his form 1040 and his evidence token to the U.S. Postal Service (USPS) Web site.

11:58 P.M., 15 April 1999: Postmark

The USPS Web server applies an electronic postmark to Joe's signed return. To apply this postmark, the USPS Web server uses its non-repudiation credential to generate an evidence token. The token contains the USPS's signature (representing a postmark), the USPS Web server's timestamp, and the USPS's certificate.

The IRS's policy requiring a postmark by midnight, 15 April, is now satisfied. Joe's policy requiring certified mail with a timestamp indicating time of submission to the USPS is also now satisfied.

12:01 A.M., 16 April 1999: Trusted Timestamp

The USPS Web server submits the postmarked document to its time server for countersignature. The USPS time server checks to make sure that the USPS timestamp is within 5 minutes of its current time and countersigns Joe's postmarked tax return. It does this by using its non-repudiation credential to generate an evidence token. The time server's evidence token contains the USPS's signature (representing a postmark), the USPS's certificate, the USPS Web server's timestamp, the USPS time server's signature, and the USPS's time server's certificate.

The USPS's policy requiring a time server's countersignature within 5 minutes of the postmark time is now satisfied.

12:01 A.M., 16 April 1999: Check USPS Web server's certificate status

The USPS may repudiate its Web server's key, but only with 30 days' advance notice, so its Web server checks to make sure its key was not repudiated before 17 March 1999 (30 days before 15 April 1999). Assuming its key is still valid, the USPS Web server uses its non-repudiation credential to transform its postmark evidence token into a complete evidence token (this will include the information that the key was not repudiated before 17 March 1999).

12:03 A.M., 16 April 1999: Check USPS time server's certificate status

The USPS may repudiate its time server's key, but only with 30 days' advance notice, so its time server checks to make sure its key was not repudiated before 17 March 1999 (30 days before 15 April 1999). Assuming its key is still valid, the USPS time server uses its non-repudiation credential to transform its countersignature evidence token into a complete evidence token (this will include the information that the key was not repudiated before 17 March 1999).

12:04 A.M., 16 April 1999: Transmit tax return and evidence tokens

Joe's tax return, Joe's signature token, the USPS's Web server's complete postmark token, and the USPS's time server's complete countersignature token are sent to the IRS server. The USPS's Web server's complete postmark token and the USPS's time server's complete countersignature token are sent to Joe.

8:17 A.M., 16 April 1999: Generate and transmit return receipt

The IRS server receives Joe's tax return. The IRS server generates a return receipt for Joe's signed tax return by countersigning it. The IRS server does this by using its non-repudiation credential to generate an evidence token. This evidence token is sent back to Joe. The IRS's evidence token is complete by definition, since the IRS's policy does not allow it to repudiate its key.

Joe's policy requiring a return receipt is now satisfied.

Arbitrating Disputes Using Non-Repudiation Evidence

Each party now has a set of non-repudiation evidence tokens. Each party can use these tokens to show that it acted properly and to verify that other parties also acted properly.

What Joe has:

Joe has his tax return and his own signature token, the USPS's complete postmark token, the USPS time server's complete countersignature token, and the IRS's complete return receipt token. Joe can use these tokens to show that he signed his tax return, that he submitted it to the post office before the midnight, 15 April deadline, and that the IRS received his signed return.

What the USPS has:

The USPS has its own complete postmark token and its own complete countersignature token. It can use these tokens to demonstrate that its postmark time was accurate to within 5 minutes.

What the IRS has:

The IRS has Joe's tax return, Joe's signature token, the USPS's complete postmark token, and the USPS's complete countersignature token. It can use Joe's token to show that he submitted the tax return, and it can use the USPS's tokens to verify that Joe's return was submitted by the midnight, 15 April deadline.

Examples of Disputes

Here's how Joe, the U.S. Postal Service, and the IRS might use evidence to help settle some disputes which might arise after Joe submits his tax return:

If the USPS loses Joe's return and then denies that it ever received it, Joe can produce his certified mail receipt as evidence that the USPS accepted the return for delivery.

If the IRS denies that it received Joe's tax return, Joe can produce his return receipt as evidence that they did receive it.

If the IRS denies that Joe submitted his return on time, Joe can produce his postmarked certified mail receipt as evidence that he mailed his return by the deadline.

If the IRS denies that the postal clerk at the USPS postmarked Joe's return with the correct time and date, the USPS can produce its time server's countersignature as evidence that its postmark time is accurate.

If Joe denies that the text of the return the IRS has is the same as what he submitted (for example, because his return was tampered with), the IRS can produce Joe's digital signature on the return as evidence that the return has not been modified.

If Joe denies that he submitted the tax return the IRS received, the IRS can produce Joe's digital signature as evidence that Joe was really the one who submitted it. But there's a problem with this evidence.

Unlike all the other evidence tokens in our example, Joe's signature token does not contain complete evidence. Remember that Joe signed his return at 11:04 P.M. on 15 April. He had to mail the return before 12:00 A.M. on 16 April. But his CA's policy gives him 48 hours to declare that his key has been compromised.

Joe could call his CA at 8:00 A.M. on 16 April and declare that his key was stolen at 8:00 A.M. on 15 April, in which case he wouldn't be liable for any signatures after that time. So Joe could claim that he mailed his real return at some other time and the IRS lost it, and that the one the IRS received on 16 April was a forgery created by the person who stole his key on 15 April.

If the IRS wanted to protect itself against this kind of fraud, it could require Joe to generate and submit a complete signature token (this would mean Joe would have to sign his return before midnight on 13 April or use another CA with a different repudiation policy).

Non-Repudiation Service Structure

In Chapter 2 we used the same picture as Figure 9-1 to illustrate how ORBs enforce security transparently, without the resource requesters and protected resources having to know anything about how security was enforced.

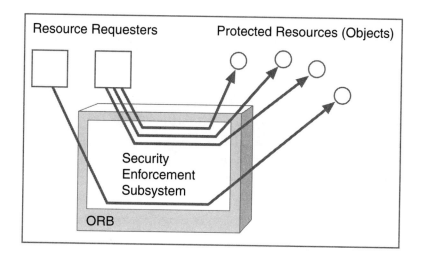

Figure 9-1
Transparent
enforcement of
security by the ORB

Unlike all the other security services we've discussed, non-repudiation can't be provided this way. Users have to know when their signature is being used to create non-repudiation evidence, for three reasons.

*Non-repudiation
can't be provided as
a transparent ORB
service*

The first reason is obvious: No user would buy a system that automatically signed his name to all kinds of documents and transactions. Imagine if your lawyer (or your kids!) signed your name to a document—without asking permission first.

The second reason is that the ORB can't know which transactions need to be signed and which don't. If I send you a draft of a contract with a couple of sections missing, I don't want to sign it, even if I'm happy with everything in the sections that are complete (because I might care about what goes in the missing sections). Later on, I might want to sign a copy of the same contract with the missing sections filled in. But my word processor isn't going to know what's supposed to go in each section of the contract or how many sections there should be. So there's no way it (or an ORB) can figure out whether the document should be signed.

*Some kinds of
non-repudiation
evidence need to be
created deliberately*

The third reason is that signatures usually aren't considered valid unless they represent the signer's intent. Even if my word processor could figure out when a document needed to be signed, any signature it applied automatically would be *its* signature and not *my* signature—because I wasn't involved in the process and couldn't have had the chance to make a decision "to sign or not to sign."

Imagine that you could convince a judge that your computer's word processor digitally signs every document it creates with your signature key, but without asking you first. Imagine that you could also convince the judge that you only recently learned that the word processor was doing all this signing behind your back. It's easy to imagine the judge throwing out a contract with your signature on it, if it was created using that word processor.

Since non-repudiation can't be provided as a transparent ORB service, CORBAsecurity provides it as an application service. Applications have to call the non-repudiation service whenever they want to generate evidence. Figure 9-2 shows how applications call the non-repudiation service.

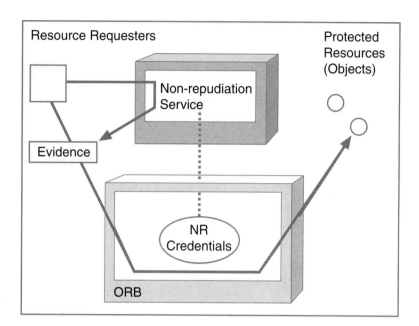

Resource Requesters

Non-repudiation
Service

Evidence

Protected
Resources
(Objects)

NR
Credentials

ORB

Figure 9-2
Non-repudiation is
an application
service

10

Questions to Ask Your Secure Object System Vendor

Question 1. What features are supported by your CORBAsecurity implementation?

The CORBAsecurity specification defines a set of *conformance levels*. Each conformance level has a set of functions which a vendor's implementation must support. When you buy a CORBAsecurity product, look carefully at the vendor's conformance statement. It will tell you whether the product you're buying has all the features you need.

You should look out for statements like "our product supports CORBAsecurity level x, features y and z"; this usually means that the vendor has implemented only a subset of the features required for CORBAsecurity conformance at the claimed level. This may be fine if features y and z are all you need, but ask questions to make sure you understand exactly what you're buying. A statement like "our product conforms to CORBAsecurity level x" means that the vendor has implemented all the features required for conformance at the claimed level.

Question 2. What is the security technology underneath your CORBAsecurity implementation?

CORBAsecurity is an interface specification. This means it describes what a CORBAsecurity implementation looks like from the outside, but not how it's built inside. Different products use different "security building blocks" to implement CORBAsecurity systems, and the choice of building blocks may affect the security of your system in important ways.

For example, if you need to transmit highly sensitive data across a network, you may want a system which uses a very strong cryptography building block to implement message protection. But if you have to transmit protected data across international borders, you may want a system with weaker cryptography so that you don't have trouble getting a license to export the system to overseas users.

The building blocks used to implement CORBAsecurity can also affect non-security aspects of your system. The choice of authentication technology, for example, can have a big effect on how easy it is to integrate CORBAsecurity with security in your other applications. If your company already uses Kerberos to authenticate users for other (non-CORBA) applications, you may want a Kerberos-based CORBAsecurity implementation, so that you don't have to create new accounts and passwords for users who need access to CORBA-based applications. If your company uses public-key certificates to authenticate users, you may prefer a public-key implementation of CORBAsecurity for the same reason.

Question 3. What assurance was done? Is the system evaluated?

A vendor's conformance statement (see Question 1) can tell you which features his product supports, but it won't tell you how well the features actually protect you. Even lists of mechanisms ("Kerberos authentication, strong cryptography," etc. . . .) won't tell you how strong a product's protection is, because a system's security is only as strong as its weakest link (and vendors aren't likely to emphasize weak links!).

The strength of a CORBAsecurity implementation's protection depends on many things, including:

- the strength of the security mechanisms (like authentication and cryptography) on which CORBAsecurity features are built
- the number of bugs in the product's code
- the security of the operating system and hardware the product runs on
- the choice of secure values for default policies

If you're using CORBAsecurity to protect very sensitive resources, you might want to get a second opinion about how secure your vendor's implementation really is. In the security world, second opinions are called "evaluations." Evaluations are based on independent analysis of a security product by an impartial third party. A number of commercial and government organizations do evaluations; you should ask your CORBAsecurity vendor for the results of any third-party evaluations of his product.

Question 4. Is the system exportable? In a full-strength version?

Because computer security and communications security technology can be used to protect intelligence data, diplomatic correspondence, and military secrets and communications, many governments classify security technology as a "munition" (like nuclear weapons), or as a "dual-use technology" (like rocket guidance systems). Many of these governments have laws restricting export (and sometimes import and use) of strong security technology—especially strong cryptographic technology.

If you need strong security, especially strong message protection, and you need to use it internationally, check very carefully with your vendor to learn the restrictions on international deployment of his product. Here are a few common situations:

- The product has relatively weak cryptography ("symmetric" or "secret" keys of less than 64 bits; "asymmetric" or "public" keys of less than about 1024 bits) but is freely exportable and usable internationally.
- The product has relatively strong cryptography and is exportable only to certain customers in certain countries, unless a special government license is obtained.
- The product comes in two versions, one with relatively strong cryptography for use in the vendor's home country, and another with relatively weak cryptography for export and international use.

Question 5. What facilities are available for managing users and privileges? Are these available to CORBA programmers? Or is administration possible only through a graphical user interface?

When the CORBAsecurity specification was written, management functions were the responsibility of a separate OMG "common facilities" working group, so user administration was left as an item for that group to define in the future. The common facilities group disbanded before user administration facilities were defined, so today's CORBAsecurity doesn't define how user accounts should be created and assigned privileges.

You should ask your CORBAsecurity vendor how his product expects you to define and manage user accounts. Here are a couple of possible answers:

- You manage accounts and privileges using the facilities of the underlying authentication system. For example, you might create users and assign them to groups using the tools provided by a Kerberos authentication server. There's no CORBA object interface to the user management functions, so CORBA programmers can't use these functions unless they create their own management objects.

- You manage accounts and privileges using a set of CORBA user management objects your CORBAsecurity vendor has defined and implemented. These support a graphical user interface and allow CORBA programs to use the management functions, but programs which call these objects probably won't work with another vendor's CORBAsecurity user management system because the user management object interfaces aren't an OMG standard.

Question 6. What facilities are available for managing assignment of new objects to domains? For moving existing objects among domains? Are these available to CORBA programmers? Or is administration possible only through a graphical user interface?

When the CORBAsecurity specification was written, management functions were the responsibility of a separate OMG "common facilities" working group, so domain membership administration was left as a future item for that group to define. The common facilities group disbanded before domain membership administration facilities were defined, so today's CORBAsecurity doesn't define how user accounts should be created and assigned privileges. OMG is in the process of specifying a standard interface for domain membership management.

You should ask your CORBAsecurity vendor how membership of objects in domains can be managed. Here are some possible answers:

- The system puts objects into domains when the objects are created; the policy that decides which objects go into which domains is defined by the vendor. Once an object has been put into a domain, it stays there.

- An administrator can define which domain an object is put into when it's created. Once an object has been put into a domain, it stays there.
- An administrator can define which domain an object is put into when it's created, and can move the object from one domain to another throughout the object's lifetime as policy requirements change.

Also ask whether your CORBAsecurity vendor is participating in the OMG process for defining the domain membership management interface standard, and whether and when the vendor's product will support that standard after it's been defined.

Question 7. What events are audited? What event channel is used? What repository is used? What audit log examination and data reduction tools are provided? Are they available to CORBA programmers?

The CORBAsecurity specification requires that implementations be able to audit principal authentication, changes to the system's security policy, setup of secure communications sessions, and access control checks.

Your vendor's implementation may also be able to audit other security-relevant events, including object invocation success or failure, changes to the security service configuration, creation and deletion of objects, and use of the non-repudiation service. Ask your vendor which events can be audited.

The CORBAsecurity specification leaves the implementation of audit event channels up to the vendor. You should ask your vendor a couple of questions about the audit event channel implementation:

- How is audit event data protected against modification while it's in the channel?

- What event disposition mechanisms does the channel support? Can alarms be raised? Can events be sent to a system management framework (for example, by generating SNMP alerts)? Can events be written into a log? Can events be discarded with no action?
- How does the channel decide how to dispose of events? Does it use a policy? Is the policy administrable?

The CORBAsecurity specification doesn't require implementations to provide an audit log as a disposition mechanism. Most implementations, however, should and will provide a log. You need to ask some questions about the log:

- How is data in the audit log protected against modification?
- How is any sensitive data in the log protected against unauthorized access?
- What facilities are provided for querying the log and/or generating reports?
- What facilities are provided for backing up and restoring the contents of the audit log?
- What happens if the log fills up? Does the system stop working? Does the system continue processing, but stop auditing? Can this be configured? Are alerts generated when the log is in danger of filling up?

Question 8. Can the system be used securely through a firewall?

Not all firewalls can be set up to allow passage of secured CORBA messages. You should ask your CORBAsecurity vendor which firewalls will allow messages secured using his product to pass through. Also ask whether the firewall needs any special configuration to allow CORBA messages to pass through it. If the firewall does need special configuration, ask whether this configuration is compatible with all the other applications you want to run through the firewall.

Question 9. What cryptography is used? Is crypto replaceable if algorithms break?

A vendor can choose from many cryptographic algorithms to protect data in a CORBAsecurity implementation. Some are stronger than others. Some aren't very strong at all, and some are of unknown quality. There are two basic types of cryptographic algorithms: symmetric (or "secret-key") and asymmetric (or "public-key"). Two basic guidelines will help you make sure that your vendor's algorithms are good, no matter whether they're secret-key or public-key.

The first thing you should look for is a standard, published algorithm. If your vendor says "we invented the algorithm ourselves," you should be worried, and investigate very carefully (get a second opinion from an expert).

Some examples of standard, published secret-key algorithms include DES, triple-DES, and RC4. Two examples of standard, published public-key algorithms are RSA and DSA. There are other good, standard, published algorithms; look in the suggested readings for a book which describes most of the popular ones.

The second thing to look for is long enough keys. For secret-key algorithms, make sure your vendor uses keys that are at least 56 bits long; this is the absolute minimum. It will protect you against casual eavesdroppers, but it probably won't protect you against a determined attack. Longer is better; if the keys are at least 80 bits long, you're probably safe against most reasonable attacks for a few years beginning in 1999. If the keys are at least 128 bits long, you're probably safe for the rest of your career (but you never know!).

For public-key algorithms, you should probably insist on keys that are at least 1024 bits long. If you can get it, 2048 is even better.

Even if your vendor has chosen a good, standard, published algorithm and a nice long key, there's always a chance someone will figure out how to break the chosen algorithm. For this reason, you should ask your vendor how hard it will be to rip out the crypto algorithm that comes with his product and put in a new one. If the answer is vague or confusing, ask for a demonstration.

Question 10. How is secure interoperability supported?

If you're going to be using ORBs and security services from more than one vendor, or if you're going to be using CORBA applications to communicate with customers and business partners who've chosen a vendor other than yours, you need to ask about interoperability. Will it be possible to send a secure message from a client using your vendor's ORB to a target object running on your business partner's chosen ORB? Will it be possible for one of your customers to send your CORBA application a secure message even if she hasn't bought a copy of your chosen ORB?

You also need to be aware that the CORBAsecurity specification defines a couple of different ways to send secure messages from one ORB to another, and they don't all provide the same level of protection.

As this book is published, OMG has defined three "secure interoperability protocols": DCE-CIOP, SECIOP, and SSL-IIOP. DCE-CIOP can provide all of the CORBAsecurity level 2 functions, but to use it you need a DCE security server.

SECIOP can also support all the CORBAsecurity level 2 functions, and it can use a wider variety of security servers than DCE-CIOP. (For example, it can use a Kerberos security server; Windows 2000 will have one of these built in.)

SSL-IIOP can't support all of the CORBAsecurity level 2 functions. (In particular, it can't support privilege attributes other than access-id, and it can't support delegation.) However, it can run on top of SSL, which is widely available.

Question 11. How is delegation supported?

Remember that there are two types of delegation: simple and compound.

Your vendor's CORBAsecurity implementation should definitely support simple delegation. If it doesn't, you won't be able to use users' identities in your access control policies if user requests ever have to go through more than one object. Make sure simple delegation is supported.

Compound delegation lets a delegate pass on its own identity along with the initiator's. You should ask whether your vendor's CORBAsecurity implementation supports compound delegation. If so, there's good news and bad news.

First, the good news: you can have a lot of control over which objects can pass messages around in your system. Now, the bad news: you will probably have to write a policy defining which objects can pass messages around in your system.

You should ask how hard it is to write the access control policy that controls which objects can be delegates in your system. Better yet, ask to see a demonstration of how delegation policy is managed. Pay close attention and ask lots of questions during the demonstration, because managing delegation policy can get *very* complicated.

Question 12. What kinds of access control policies are supported? How can they be combined?

CORBAsecurity level 2 requires implementations to support the access control system we discussed in this book (it's called domain-AccessPolicy). This policy system may or may not be just what you need.

You should ask your vendor whether other access control policy systems are supported. Also ask whether a single object can be protected by more than one policy at the same time (and whether it can be protected by more than one kind of policy at the same time).

If objects can be protected by more than one policy, there will probably be rules for deciding which policy "wins" if different policies "disagree." (That is, if one policy says access should be granted and another says access should be denied.) Ask what these rules are.

Question 13. Is label-based access control supported?

Some kinds of systems label data to make sure it's handled correctly. Medical record-keeping systems label some kinds of data (HIV status and mental health information, for example) to make sure it's kept private. Military systems label classified data to make sure it isn't shown to people who don't have a "need to know." Web servers sometimes use "content labels" to help people avoid data which might offend them.

If you have (or need) an application with security-related data labels, ask your vendor whether his CORBAsecurity implementation can use data labels to make access control decisions. You should also ask what kinds of labels are supported (to make sure that the labels you want to use will be OK).

Suggested Reading

If you want to find out more about security or object-oriented technology, here are a few books you may want to take a look at.

Amoroso, E., *Fundamentals of Computer Security Technology*, Prentice Hall, 1994.

This is a broad introduction to the concepts behind computer security for people who are thinking about becoming security professionals. It's fairly short and is well written, but it's intended for a technical audience, so you'll need to pay attention.

Gollmann, D., *Computer Security*, John Wiley & Sons, 1999.

This is my favorite introduction to security. It's very practical and balanced; it includes a large dose of historical background on the subjects it covers; and it has an excellent bibliography. It also covers a very broad range of important topics without getting bogged down in detail. Again, it's intended for a technical audience.

Kaufman, C., Perlman, R., and Speciner, M., *Network Security: Private Communication in a Public World*, Prentice Hall, 1995.

In addition to being the best description of network security protocols available, this book wins my vote for "most entertaining technical book of the decade." It's clear, comprehensive, and accurate—and very funny in many places. It's intended for a technical audience.

Kippenhahn, R., *Code Breaking: A History and Exploration*, Overlook Press, 1999.

This book, recently translated from the German original, is a highly readable short history of codes and codebreaking. There are lots of fascinating stories, among which the author sneaks in technical descriptions of how cryptographic algorithms work. The book is intended for a general audience in spite of the occasional technical content.

Menezes, A., Van Oorschot, P., and Vanstone, S., *Handbook of Applied Cryptography*, CRC Press, 1996.

My favorite cryptography reference. Extremely clear, careful presentations of all the important current cryptographic algorithms. Highly technical and mathematical.

Russell, D. and Gangemi, G., *Computer Security Basics*, O'Reilly & Associates, 1991.

This book is getting a little dated, but there's still nothing better as an introduction to security for nontechnical audiences. This is the place to start if you're interested in a broad (but not too deep) introduction to security technology and you don't have a lot of technical or mathematical background.

Soley, R. and Stone, C., *Object Management Architecture Guide*, 3rd edition, John Wiley & Sons, 1996.

The official bible of OMG's CORBA technology. CORBA is always being updated by the OMG working groups, so this should be considered a starting point. After you've read this, you should go to the OMG's web page (www.omg.org) and look for the latest developments.

Taylor, D., *Object Technology: A Manager's Guide, Second Edition*, Addison Wesley Longman, 1997.

The best introduction to object technology I know of. Short, crystal-clear, and highly readable, it focuses on the important ideas and leaves the details for other works. Can be read in an afternoon.

Glossary

access control: the security service which guards protected resources against unauthorized access.

access control check: the security function which decides whether a subject's request to perform an action on a protected resource should be granted or denied.

access identity: a non-public security attribute describing a subject's unique access control identity.

accessDecision: the CORBAsecurity interface used to request an access control check.

accountability: the security service which records who did what, when, so that users can be held responsible for their actions.

action: an object's response to a method invocation; initiators send messages to objects asking them to perform actions.

assurance: work done by the builder of a system to ensure that the system keeps its security promises.

assurance argument: a system vendor's attempt to convince the customer that a system keeps its security promises.

assurance evidence: data which supports a vendor's claim that a system keeps its security promises.

attribute: a piece of data inside an object.

audit: the process of checking a system to see whether it is secure.

audit channel: the security function which disposes of audit events. Newly generated audit events are placed in the audit channel, and the audit channel disposes of them by placing them into a log, generating alarms, deleting them, or doing something else.

audit event: the system's record of a security-relevant system event.

audit selector: the audit policy rule which defines whether a particular type of system event should result in the generation of an audit event.

auditChannel: the CORBAsecurity interface used to generate and dispose of audit events.

auditDecision: the CORBAsecurity interface used to decide whether an audit event should be generated when a system event occurs.

authentication: the security service which requires users to prove their identities.

authorization: the security service which guards protected resources against unauthorized access.

availability: the property of a system that it is able to respond to requests in a timely fashion.

class: the recipe for creating an object. A class consists of a set of interfaces.

clearance: a non-public security attribute describing a subject's entitlement to perform actions on sensitive data protected using sensitivity labels.

compound delegation: the security function by which a delegate passes its own credentials together with the received credentials of an initiator to the next intermediate in a delegation chain.

confidentiality: the security function which protects sensitive data against disclosure to unauthorized users.

CORBA: "Common Object Request Broker Architecture." OMG's standard for object-oriented middleware. See "ORB."

CORBAsecurity: the OMG standard describing how to secure CORBA environments.

countermeasure: a procedure, action, or device used to reduce the risk caused by a threat.

credential: the container for a subject's security attributes.

Current: the CORBA object which stores the data (including credentials) related to an execution context.

delegate: an intermediate in a delegation chain which acts on behalf of the initiator of a request.

delegation: the security function which allows one subject to act on another's behalf.

delegation chain: a sequence of subjects cooperating to process a single request. A delegation chain's first member is the initiator of the request. The request may be passed to one or more intermediates, each of whom may choose to become a delegate by acting on the initiator's behalf. The last intermediate in a delegation chain passes the request to its target.

digital signature: a piece of encrypted data which provides evidence that a specific subject performed an action on a specific piece of data.

disaster recovery: the security function which gets a system back up and running after a service interruption.

domain: a collection of objects. CORBAsecurity manages policy using domains; each domain is assigned a policy, which is applied to all the members of the domain.

encapsulation: the property of an object which hides the details of its implementation and its data from its callers.

encryption: the security function which transforms data into an unintelligible form.

evidence: data which supports a claim. See: assurance evidence, non-repudiation evidence.

execution context: the collection of information a system uses to keep track of one subject's use of one copy of one program.

group: a non-public security attribute describing an arbitrary collection of subjects.

identification: the security function which allows subjects to claim identities. Most secure systems require subjects to use authentication to prove the identities they claim through identification.

identity: a non-public security attribute which is unique to a single subject.

initiator: (1) the subject which generates a request by sending a message. (2) the first subject in a delegation chain.

instance: an individual object, created by instantiating a class.

instantiation: the process of creating an object (called an instance) using the recipe in a specified class.

integrity: the security function which protects sensitive data against modification by unauthorized users.

interface: a description of the set of methods and the set of attributes which an object contains. A class is a set of one or more interfaces.

intermediate: a subject in a delegation chain which is neither the initiator nor the target of the request. An intermediate which chooses to act on behalf of the initiator becomes a delegate.

invocation credential: a credential which will represent an initiator's identity the next time a message is initiated from the current execution context. By default the own credential of the subject who created the current execution context is used as the invocation credential; a subject can use a received credential as its invocation credential by calling the delegation service.

message: a initiator's request for a target object to perform an action.

message origin authentication: the security function which proves the identity of an initiator to a target.

message protection: the security function which protects the authenticity, integrity, and confidentiality of a message.

method: a function an object can perform. See interface.

non-repudiation: the security service which generates evidence of subjects' actions.

non-repudiation evidence: data which supports the claim that a particular subject performed a particular action on a particular object.

object: (1) object-oriented usage: an instance of a class (2) security usage: a resource to which protection can be applied by defining policy.

OMG: "Object Management Group." An organization which defines vendor-neutral standards for object-oriented technology.

ORB: "Object Request Broker." The middleware which allows initiators to send messages to target objects.

own credential: a credential which represents the identity of the subject who created an execution context.

policy: the rules which describe how a secure system will protect resources.

principal authentication: the security function which allows subjects to acquire non-public security attributes (identities and privileges).

principalAuthenticator: the CORBA object which performs principal authentication and creates credentials.

privilege: a non-public security attribute which is not (necessarily) unique to a single subject.

protected resource: resources for which policies have been defined.

protection: defends a system against threats by implementing countermeasures.

public: the security attribute which all subjects are entitled to, even if they do not authenticate themselves.

QOP (Quality of Protection): the type and strength of authenticity, confidentiality, and integrity protection applied to a message.

received credential: a credential in the execution context of the receiver of a request which represents the identity of the initiator of the request.

reference: the unique value an ORB uses to locate an object.

required rights: the rights necessary to invoke a particular method of a particular interface. CORBAsecurity defines four rights: "get," "set," "manage," and "use."

requiredRights: the CORBAsecurity object which defines the required rights for each interface in a system.

role: a non-public security attribute describing a collection of subjects who perform the same job function.

security attribute: an adjective used to describe a subject's security-relevant characteristics. There are two general classes of security attributes: identities and privileges.

securityContext: the CORBAsecurity object which implements message protection.

service continuity: the security function which protects a system against the threat of service interruption.

simple delegation: the security function by which a delegate passes an initiator's received credential (instead of its own credential) to the next intermediate in a delegation chain.

subject: an active entity in a system; has an independent will

system event: anything that happens in a system.

target: the intended recipient of a message.

threat: a bad thing which might happen in (or to) a system.

transparent: the property of a service which can be provided to applications or objects without their knowledge.

Index

Note to the reader: Illustrations are indicated by *italicized* page numbers.

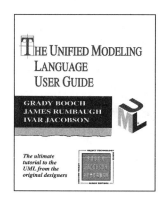

The Unified Modeling Language User Guide

Grady Booch, James Rumbaugh, and Ivar Jacobson
Addison-Wesley Object Technology Series

The Unified Modeling Language User Guide is a two-color introduction to the core eighty percent of the Unified Modeling Language, approaching it in a layered fashion and showing the application of the UML to modeling problems across a wide variety of application domains. This landmark book is suitable for developers unfamiliar with the UML or modeling in general, and will also be useful to experienced developers who wish to learn how to apply the UML to advanced problems.

0-201-57168-4 • Hardcover • 512 pages • ©1999

Surviving Object-Oriented Projects

A Manager's Guide
Alistair Cockburn
Addison-Wesley Object Technology Series

This book allows you to survive and ultimately succeed with an object-oriented project. Alistair Cockburn draws on his personal experience and extensive knowledge to provide the information that managers need to combat the unforeseen challenges that await them during project implementation. *Surviving Object-Oriented Projects* supports its key points through short case studies taken from real object-oriented projects. In addition, an appendix collects these guidelines and solutions into brief "crib sheets" that are ideal for handy reference.

0-201-49834-0 • Paperback • 272 pages • ©1998

Doing Hard Time

Developing Real-Time Systems with UML, Objects, Frameworks, and Patterns
Bruce Powel Douglass
Addison-Wesley Object Technology Series

Doing Hard Time is written to facilitate the daunting process of developing real-time systems. The author presents an embedded systems programming methodology that has been proved successful in practice. The process outlined in this book allows application developers to apply practical techniques—garnered from the mainstream areas of object-oriented software development—to meet the demanding qualifications of real-time programming.

0-201-49837-5 • Hardcover • 800 pages • ©1999

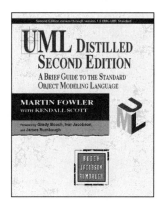

UML Distilled, Second Edition
A Brief Guide to the Standard Object Modeling Language
Martin Fowler with Kendall Scott
Addison-Wesley Object Technology Series

Thoroughly revised and updated, this best-selling book is a concise overview that introduces you to the Unified Modeling Language, highlighting the key elements of the standard modeling language's notation, semantics, and processes. Included is a brief explanation of the UML's history, development, and rationale, as well as discussions on how the UML can be integrated into the object-oriented development process. The book also profiles various modeling techniques associated with UML—use cases, CRC cards, design by contract, dynamic classification, interfaces, and abstract classes. The first edition of this classic work was named recipient of *Software Development* magazine's 1997 Productivity Award.

0-201-65783-X • Paperback • 224 pages • ©2000

Advanced CORBA Programming with C++
Michi Henning and Steve Vinoski
Addison-Wesley Professional Computing Series

Here is the CORBA book that every C++ software engineer has been waiting for. This book provides designers and developers with the tools required to understand CORBA technology at the architectural, design, and source code levels. The authors offer hands-on explanations for building efficient applications, as well as lucid examples that provide practical advice on avoiding costly mistakes.

0-201-37927-9 • Paperback • 1120 pages • ©1999

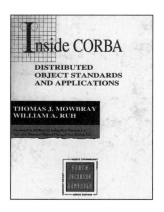

Inside CORBA
Distributed Object Standards and Applications
Thomas J. Mowbray and William A. Ruh
Addison-Wesley Object Technology Series

Inside CORBA is a comprehensive, up-to-date, and authoritative guide to distributed object architecture, software development, and CORBA standards. It includes the latest coverage of the new CORBA IDL Language Mapping for the Java programming language and comprehensive coverage of the CORBA 2 standard and CORBA services. The authors outline essential lessons learned from experienced CORBA managers and architects to ensure successful adoption and migration to CORBA technology.

0-201-89540-4 • Paperback • 400 pages • ©1997

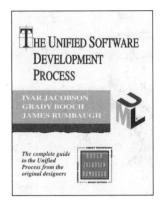

The Unified Software Development Process

Ivar Jacobson, Grady Booch, and James Rumbaugh
Addison-Wesley Object Technology Series

The Unified Software Development Process goes beyond other object-oriented analysis and design methods by detailing a family of processes that incorporate the complete lifecycle of software development. This new book, representing the collaboration of Ivar Jacobson, Grady Booch, and James Rumbaugh, clearly describes the different higher-level constructs—notation as well as semantics—used in the models. Thus stereotypes such as use cases and actors, packages, classes, interfaces, active classes, processes and threads, nodes, and most relations are described intuitively in the context of a model.

0-201-57169-2 • Hardcover • 512 pages • ©1999

The Rational Unified Process

An Introduction
Philippe Kruchten
Addison-Wesley Object Technology Series

This concise book offers a quick introduction to the concepts, structure, content, and motivation of the Rational Unified Process. This revolutionary software development process provides a disciplined approach to assigning, managing, and completing tasks within a software development organization and is the first development process to exploit the full capabilities of the industry-standard Unified Modeling Language. The Rational Unified Process is unique in that it captures many of the proven best practices in modern software development and presents them in a form that can be tailored to a wide range of projects and organizations.

0-201-60459-0 • Paperback • 272 pages • ©1999

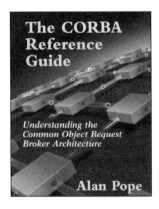

The CORBA Reference Guide

Understanding the Common Object Request Broker Architecture
Alan Pope

This book offers a clear explanation of CORBA as well as a complete reference to the standard. *The CORBA Reference Guide* provides a general background in distributed systems and explains the base architecture as well as the services and facilities that extend this architecture. Of particular note, the book details the most sophisticated security framework that has been developed for any architecture to date and covers interoperability with other ORBs.

0-201-63386-8 • Paperback • 432 pages • ©1998

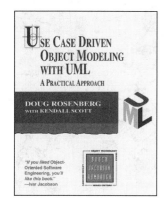

Use Case Driven Object Modeling with UML
A Practical Approach
Doug Rosenberg with Kendall Scott
Addison-Wesley Object Technology Series

This book presents a streamlined approach to UML modeling that includes a minimal but sufficient set of diagrams and techniques you can use to get from use cases to code quickly and efficiently. *Use Case Driven Object Modeling with UML* provides practical guidance that will allow software developers to produce UML models quickly and efficiently, while maintaining traceability from user requirements through detailed design and coding. The authors draw on their extensive industry experience to present proven methods for driving the object modeling process forward from use cases in a simple and straight-forward manner.

0-201-43289-7 • Paperback • 192 pages • ©1999

IIOP Complete
Understanding CORBA and Middleware Interoperability
William Ruh, Thomas Herron, and Paul Klinker
Addison-Wesley Object Technology Series

The Internet Inter-ORB Protocol (IIOP) was designed to allow disparate software components to communicate with one another, and ensures interoperability on top of the most popular communications protocol in use today—TCP/IP. While IIOP is a specialized subset of the broader CORBA specification, its popularity is increasing steadily. This book provides a broad perspective of IIOP, allowing any CORBA developer to gain an in-depth understanding of the foundational standard. In turn, an increased knowledge of IIOP allows systems developers to more easily build interoperable objects for the enterprise.

0-201-37925-2 • Paperback • 272 pages • ©2000

The Unified Modeling Language Reference Manual
James Rumbaugh, Ivar Jacobson, and Grady Booch
Addison-Wesley Object Technology Series

James Rumbaugh, Ivar Jacobson, and Grady Booch have created the definitive reference to the UML. This two-color book covers every aspect and detail of the UML and presents the modeling language in a useful reference format that serious software architects or programmers should have on their bookshelf. The book is organized by topic and designed for quick access. The authors also provide the necessary information to enable existing OMT, Booch, and OOSE notation users to make the transition to UML. The text also includes an overview of the semantic foundation of the UML in a concise appendix.

0-201-30998-X • Hardcover with CD-ROM • 576 pages • ©1999

Addison-Wesley Computer and Engineering Publishing Group

How to Interact with Us

1. Visit our Web site

http://www.awl.com/cseng

When you think you've read enough, there's always more content for you at Addison-Wesley's web site. Our web site contains a directory of complete product information including:

- Chapters
- Exclusive author interviews
- Links to authors' pages
- Tables of contents
- Source code

You can also discover what tradeshows and conferences Addison-Wesley will be attending, read what others are saying about our titles, and find out where and when you can meet our authors and have them sign your book.

2. Subscribe to Our Email Mailing Lists

Subscribe to our electronic mailing lists and be the first to know when new books are publishing. Here's how it works: Sign up for our electronic mailing at http://www.awl.com/cseng/mailinglists.html. Just select the subject areas that interest you and you will receive notification via email when we publish a book in that area.

3. Contact Us via Email

cepubprof@awl.com

Ask general questions about our books.
Sign up for our electronic mailing lists.
Submit corrections for our web site.

bexpress@awl.com

Request an Addison-Wesley catalog.
Get answers to questions regarding
your order or our products.

innovations@awl.com

Request a current Innovations Newsletter.

webmaster@awl.com

Send comments about our web site.

jcs@awl.com

Submit a book proposal.
Send errata for an Addison-Wesley book.

cepubpublicity@awl.com

Request a review copy for a member of the media
interested in reviewing new Addison-Wesley titles.

We encourage you to patronize the many fine retailers who stock Addison-Wesley titles. Visit our online directory to find stores near you or visit our online store: http://store.awl.com/ or call 800-824-7799.

Addison Wesley Longman
Computer and Engineering Publishing Group
One Jacob Way, Reading, Massachusetts 01867 USA
TEL 781-944-3700 • FAX 781-942-3076